The Drama Teacher's Survival Guide #2

Activities, exercises and techniques for the theatre classroom

Margaret F. Johnson

MERIWETHER PUBLISHING
A division of Pioneer Drama Service, Inc.
Denver, Colorado

Meriwether Publishing
A division of Pioneer Drama Service, Inc.
PO Box 4267
Englewood, CO 80155

www.pioneerdrama.com

Editor: Theodore O. Zapel
Assistant editor: Amy Hammelev
Cover design: Jan Melvin

The Library of Congress has cataloged the paperback version as follows:

Johnson, Margaret (Margaret Friedl)
   The drama teacher's survival guide #2 : activities, exercises, and techniques for the theatre classroom / by Margaret F. Johnson. -- 1st ed.
       p. cm.
     ISBN 978-1-56608-182-5 (pbk.)
    1. Drama--Study and teaching (Secondary) I. Title.
    PN1701.J642   2011
    792.071'2--dc23
                                   2011020471

Contents

Acknowledgments and Credits

First, a big thank you to the folks at Meriwether Publishing and Contemporary Drama for all their help: Ted, Mark, and especially Amy. I again want to thank my faithful readers: Tammi Allison, Georgiana Graf, Michele Nokleby, and particularly Tom Valach.

Without my wonderful students at Sentinel High School, those talented kids from the Missoula Children's Theatre Fine Arts Camp, and my new students from the Osher Lifelong Learning Institute at the University of Montana, this book would never have been possible. A special thank you to the following students for allowing me to use their work: Scott Michael Campbell, Andrew Copley, Nicholas Daue, Johanna Dreiling, Ben Erickson, Brittney McLaughlin, Brian Theroux, and Arielle Nachtigal for playing Sally Glutz.

To my husband, thanks for all your love, support, photographs used in this book, and the grand adventure that is our family life together. Thank You!

Introduction

Greetings! You are so excited to start teaching drama, sharing your love and excitement of this truly creative course. So, where do you start and what can you do in a drama class? You can start anywhere, with just about anything theatrical, from technical theatre to pantomime, improvisation to writing a student-directed show. Much of what you will be teaching depends on your specific area of expertise and your background. You will also have to take into consideration your school's educational philosophy as well as your state's theatre guidelines.

What can you do? This book includes various suggestions for a drama classroom that I want to share with you. Having taught high school theatre for thirty-seven years, I collected many drama activities, exercises, handouts, lessons, and techniques that I found extremely successful and enjoyable to teach. This is by no means a complete drama course, but rather eight units my students needed to know and experience to thoroughly understand and appreciate the wonderful world of theatre.

Philosophy of Teaching

Before I go any further, it is important to state my philosophy about teaching drama.

Group Work

I was a firm believer in group activities because theatre is not about one person's individual performance (with the exception of monologues), but rather a variety of actors sharing a common experience. You will notice that the majority of the activities and exercises are group oriented.

Enjoying Theatre after High School

I did not go into teaching theatre with the idea that I would "create" great Hollywood or Broadway actors or technicians. I wanted my students to enjoy being onstage, take pride in what they accomplished, and hopefully attend theatrical productions throughout their lives, appreciating and understanding the hours spent on the production. There is a joy about being in an audience, which is so much more rewarding than going to a movie or watching TV. It is like attending a grand wedding or an outstanding performance. It is a shared experience. And my students might even get involved in community theatre.

    One of my many pleasures in retirement is having the opportunity to work with former students in our community theatre. I recently was directed by one of my "kids" in *Arsenic and Old Lace,* a very successful production. He was a joy to work with, as were two of the other characters, who were also my "kids."

    Check out my April, 2011, blog for an article written in our local paper: http://contemporarydramanewsletter.contemporary drama.com/public/blog/203097

Creating a Safe Environment

I never wanted my students to be "put on the spot" or to feel self-conscious. I wanted them to become very comfortable, feel safe, and trust the other students in the class. Before I worked on solo activities, we all needed to experience working with each other in the class, creating a feeling of family. My students became my "kids." Theatre is about family and your classroom has to instill this feeling before your students are willing to risk, yes risk, getting up and performing.

I will never forget an advanced drama class in the early 90s. We were writing scenes for our show, described in Unit 8. I had the privilege of working with several boys in the class for three years. They were inseparable. We were also producing Tim Kelly's musical *Blue Suede Paws*. One of the songs in the show was "To Thine Ownself Be True."

When Bob began his two-person scene with his best friend Zeb, he said that this was a very serious piece — he had always been the class clown — and Zeb was reading the following piece cold.

Two Best Friends

(BOB and ZEB are fishing. BOB seems preoccupied and ZEB is in a relatively happy mood.)

ZEB: Oh, I brought Beth to my house last night after the movie to meet my mom. My mom said she wants to meet whoever I go to prom with since she's paying for my tux.

BOB: Oh ... that's cool.

ZEB: So are you going to ask Kathy to the prom or not?

BOB: Ah ... I don't know. I might have to work that night.

ZEB: Dude, it's two months away. Man, I can't believe you didn't nail her last weekend. She was all over you.

BOB: Well, I had to take her home.

ZEB: Did you even kiss her?

BOB: NO! Well, no way man. She's a dog.

ZEB: WHAT! Kathy Baker is the hottest girl in the school and she gives it up, too. What more could you ask for?

BOB: Well, I'm not that shallow ... I mean, maybe I want more than just that. *(Pauses, ZEB stares at BOB.)*

ZEB: Dude, sometimes I wonder about you man, you're nuts ... I just don't get it.

BOB: No, you don't get it.

ZEB: What's that supposed to mean?!?

BOB: Never mind. *(Pause)*

ZEB: Is something bugging you? I mean I can tell something's on your mind. I wish you'd just talk about it.

BOB: Just never mind. *(Pause)* How well do you think you know me?

ZEB: I've known you my whole life. I mean, I know everything about you.

BOB: Well, if you know everything about me, what about me makes you want to be friends with me?

ZEB: Oh, I don't know. You're just a cool person to be around. I mean, we're going fishing and we do everything else together. Why else are people friends?

BOB: Would you change your opinion on me if you found out something bad about me? *(Pause)*

ZEB: Did you kill somebody?

BOB: ... No, it wouldn't be anything that affects anyone else. It's just me.

ZEB: Well, I mean, even if you did kill someone, I'd still be your friend.

BOB: ... What if I told you I was gay.

ZEB: *(ZEB stares at BOB then suddenly looks away — nervously)* Ahh ... *(Squirming)* Oh ... *(Start laugh)* That was pretty good. You really had me going ... I mean you ... *(ZEB looks at BOB and sees that he is serious.)* Oh ... Oh shoot.

BOB: Does that change your opinion about me? *(Pause)* I mean, I know it's a shock, but I can't keep it a secret any more.

ZEB: Well, ah, why do you want to be a fag ... I mean gay?

BOB: Well, I never chose it. It's something I can't help. Ya know. I guess I was just born this way.

ZEB: Oh ... I just believe it, I mean, I guess if it's just part of you and you can't help it then I can't really judge you on it ... Do you have AIDS?

BOB: NO! *(Laugh)*

ZEB: Have you ever ... *(Awkward)* ya know, ... ah ... done things?

BOB: NO!

ZEB: Then how do ya know that you're ...

BOB: Gay?

ZEB: Yeah.

BOB: Well, how do you know that you're straight? I mean it's just the way you feel ... Oh and I don't want you to think I'm friends with you for any other reason, but just friends. Ya know.

ZEB: Oh, I know. My mom is friends with a gay guy and he's pretty cool, but, I mean, you're not going to start talking like a girl or anything are you? *(He does.)*

BOB: Ick. No. I'm not like that. I'm the same person now as I was before I told you.

ZEB: Well, I'm glad you told me. It took a lot of guts and you'll still be my friend. I always thought that gay guys acted weird but you're just a normal guy.

BOB: That's why I told you, 'cause I knew you'd be mature enough to handle it. We don't have to dwell on it; I mean, it won't change nothin'. I just wanted you to know everything about me so I wouldn't have to go around lying to you and acting like someone I'm not.

ZEB: I've always been taught that being gay is bad, and gross, but you're normal and you haven't changed at all to me.

BOB: Thanks.

ZEB: Come on. Let's go catch some fish.

Needless to say the class was stunned *and* very accepting. Bob had not even told his parents. He said, "I could not continue living a lie and sing the song, 'To Thine Ownself Be True.'" We all felt so honored that he was willing to open his heart to us. It was a very special moment and I have never forgotten it.

It was agreed that his piece, though well written, was not appropriate for our teenage show. Yes, it was/is a problem teenagers face, but at the time, we felt it was too touchy a subject for our show.

High Expectations

I held all of my students and myself to an incredibly high standard. I would accept nothing but the best from each of my students. I knew that they were capable of great things and I accepted nothing less. And in return, I tried to give my best day in and day out, leading by example.

Did my students think I didn't like them? Did I frustrate them? Did I yell at them? Yes, of course. Below is a true experience of a sophomore my final year of teaching that illustrates this perfectly.

> I remember the bone chilling fear I had of going on tasks for Mrs. J ...
>
> MRS. J: Cory, would you go upstairs and get the extension cord out of my classroom? It's in the corner by the scripts. Please do this very simple task for me.
>
> CORY: Okay. *(Starts upstairs.) Shoot!* The extension cord isn't there ... There must be another corner where the scripts are ... *shoot, shoot!* There's no other corner! Oh my god, I can't go back empty handed, the life of this very production is teetering on my ability to locate a stupid cord so that we can plug in a dang stereo two feet further away from the wall ... *(Breaking into a cold sweat)* ... dang it! ... I've got it! I'll unplug everything off Mrs. Johnson's desk and bring down her surge protector with multiple outlets. Maybe that will stretch long enough. *Perfect!*
>
> MRS. J: *(From below) CCCCooooorrrryyyyy!*

Most of my students came to realize that the frustration and yelling was not because I disliked them but because they were shortchanging themselves, not living up to their potential. I'm not saying you should spend the hours I did, put the fear of the almighty, or even shout at your students, but what I am saying is, "Do not settle for mediocrity. Expect much more of your students and they will rise up to your expectations."

Assignments

I would often demonstrate an activity, but sometimes I loved to just explain it and see what the class created on their own. I felt that if they had to figure out how to do the activity, it became theirs and not a copy of the teacher's example.

I believed there is no correct way to do an activity. There may be a funnier way, a sadder way, or a more dramatic way, but no absolute right way. That is what makes theatre an art, a truly creative outlet, and a pleasure to teach. I also believed that my students needed to:

- Say, "I'll try," rather than, "No," or "I can't do that." If they had not prepared an assignment, a simple, "I didn't do it" was preferred to any other excuse. I could not, and would not, tolerate a liar.
- Respect each other and themselves.
- Give constructive criticism rather than negatively criticize each other's performances.
- Ask any questions or make comments about a given activity at the beginning or end of the lesson. Once an activity began, those not involved directly were to watch, be a good audience, and wait until it was completed before questioning.

Sources

I acquired these ideas from many sources — organizing, adding, and changing them to fit my program. I have taken numerous college courses, have a dog-eared copy of Viola Spolin's book *Improvisation for the Theatre,* attended a Brian Way workshop, bought many books on improvisation including Justine Jones and Mary Ann Kelley's *Improv Ideas,* and have scoured the Internet. Many of these activities are my own invention, but just as many I have modified through trial and error.

Lessons for Substitute Teachers

This book could also come in handy if you need lesson plans for a substitute. It not only will help you in your planning ahead but will save you time by not having to write out everything for someone who has a very limited background in theatre. I know how hard it is to find qualified subs; horrible things can and do happen.

I have had substitutes just sit at my desk and knit, letting my students do "whatever." Another totally reorganized my desk and bookshelves. I could find nothing on my return! And yet another brought his own lesson plans, writing jingles, which had nothing to do with drama!

One of my student teachers, who now has a wonderful program at her school, was attending her father's funeral in another state and needed a sub for the week. On the day of the funeral she received a phone call from one of her student's parents, apologizing profusely for bothering her on such a sad occasion, but wanted her to know that her sub had asked her students, in each of her drama classes, to act out a "private" body part in front of the class. Needless to say, she called her principal and had the sub replaced. No teacher, or anyone for that matter, should have to be confronted with such a situation.

A Final Note

I hope you find this select group of activities, exercises, handouts, lessons, and techniques for the drama classroom helpful and fun to teach. Delight in what your students can accomplish. Remember, theatre enriches our lives and teaching theatre is not only a joy, but a privilege. You never know whom you will inspire: maybe a costumer or designer, a future drama teacher, a Broadway actress, or even the CEO of the Prime Time Emmys!

Unit 1
The First Week

As my students entered my classroom, I welcomed them, gave them a quick overview of what we were going to be accomplishing for the semester or year, and told them just a bit about myself. I did not give them my life history, but something about my background in theatre as well as my education, maybe two minutes worth. I then got down to business by talking about my requirements. I required a notebook that included four handouts: Grade Sheet, Productions Around Missoula, Basic Critique Format, and, of course, the Course Management and Content. Why did I think these were so important?

Course Management and Content

After getting your room ready for your new students, you need to prepare your Course Management and Content along with a course outline. Not only does it help you get organized and give students your expectations, but it may be mandated by your administration. Make this simple, allowing room for the school's policies as well as the course content and expectations you think are important. Be sure your students understand this information. Sometimes I even gave a little bonus quiz over the "good stuff."

Grades

When I was in school, grades were a *big secret!* All of my teachers guarded their grade books with their lives, locking them in their desks. We were never privy to any information until the report cards came out. I realize in today's world parents can email you or visit the school's website to get grade information; however, most of my teaching career was the time before computers and grade programs, so I created a form, a grade book of sorts, so at any time my students or their parents could access their grades. Just be sure your students' and their parents are aware of their progress in your classes and there are no misunderstandings.

I used the point system, which corresponded to the school district's grading policy, rather than percentages for my grades. Numbers were much easier for me to work with. When an assignment was very important, I assigned it a higher number of points. As our district changed its requirements, I changed my point system to match.

Productions around Your Community

I felt it was very important as we were talking, reading, and doing theatre that my students see plays. We all know plays are written to be staged and seeing theatre enriches our lives. I wanted my students to see live theatre, using their classroom knowledge to analyze productions they attended, but first I had to get them into those theatre seats.

I required my drama students to see our productions, and it was equally important they see shows produced by others, whether it be another high school, university, traveling show, church, or community theatre. Creating a form called Productions Around Missoula that included dates, titles, locations, and curtain times of every production in Missoula, ensured that all my students knew what was happening theatrically around Missoula.

I always stipulated that if they did not have the money to go to the play, I would be very happy to provide them with a ticket. Not doing this part of their class requirements because they didn't have money was not an option.

Theatre Behavior

Before my students started working in class on our various activities, I spent time talking about being a good audience. As stated in the introduction, my students needed to:

- Respect each other and themselves.
- Give constructive criticism rather than negatively criticize each other's performances.
- Ask any questions or make comments about a given activity at the beginning or end of the lesson. Once an activity began, those not involved directly were to watch, be a good audience, and wait until it was completed before questioning.

When the first play was being performed, I discussed the differences between our classroom activities and going to a theatre. As we had practiced being courteous in class, this was just an extension of what they did every day. The following speech certainly could be made into a handout. I chose to spend time in class to go over all the points so there was no question of what was expected when attending a performance.

Theatre Etiquette Lesson/Speech

Power is a fascinating thing. Attending a play gives you a great deal of power — the power, as an audience, to help make a success or a failure of each production. It is a responsibility not to be taken lightly.

Every production represents a great deal of time, at least some money, and countless hours of hard work by actors, directors, and technicians. Their effort deserves a respectful audience. (When we were producing our shows, I would go into great detail about this information.) Not every audience member sees a performance in the same way. Some of us are fond of musical theatre, some like comedy, some drama. Many prefer contemporary plays, while others like classical theatre. No matter what type of theatre is your favorite, each deserves your courteous and full attention.

If you're unfamiliar with a show you're going to see, ask about it. (Again, when I gave out the dates for specific productions, which they recorded in Plays Around Missoula, I would take time to discuss each one. Even if I felt the show was inappropriate for the students, I would talk about it with the caveat that they had to have their parent's permission to see it.) You do not have to like the production, but the production deserves to have a respectful audience. Your likes and dislikes can be covered in your critiques.

There are several things to keep in mind about the rules in a theatre:

- Keep feet off the seats of the auditorium.
- No eating, drinking, texting, or smoking in the auditorium.
- Turn off your watch alarms, beepers, cell phones, etc.
- No photographs during performances.
- If you must leave the theatre during a show, leave *quietly* during a blackout or a scene change.
- Talking in the audience or any other disruptive behavior is unforgivable.
- Show your excitement with applause and respond to the actors rather than discuss the show while it's in progress with your friends.

Please remember the time to discuss and evaluate the performance is after it's over. (On several occasions our student audiences were very unruly, once with a laser pointer and others with loud disruptions, which I would not tolerate. I went onstage, stopped the show, and told them to return to their respective classes. "The show was over!" It was a hard lesson for those who were good audience members, but believe me, I got my message across.)

Applause is the audience's way of giving back some of the energy the actors have given them, and it's important to let performers know when their good work is appreciated. But applause can be overdone. Not every funny line should be interrupted with a thunderous outburst of clapping. Inappropriate applause can hinder a performance, especially a good one, as much as it can help it.

Standing ovations, the ultimate compliment of the show, should be reserved for the very best. If you stand up for every show, how will you express your pleasure and respect when you see a piece of theatre that is really powerful and moving? A little restraint is in order here.

Basic Critique Format

How did I know they had seen a production? By requiring a written essay much like the five paragraph theme. Not only was I assured they had seen the play (about 98% of the time I was assured they had seen the play, but I also know I was hoodwinked on several occasions!), but it also made writing a key component of my curriculum. The Basic Critique Format requirements I handed out to my students are listed below.

- The critique is due the first Monday after the last performance, at the beginning of the period. If the last performance is on Sunday, the critique is due first thing on Tuesday.
- You must have a program. You must also have a rough draft stapled to the back of the final draft showing evidence of changes from the rough draft. I am not interested in a rough draft that is a carbon copy of the final draft! The ticket stub is stapled to the front of the final draft. The stapled critique must be inserted into the program. If a ticket and/or program are not issued, explain why in the first paragraph of your critique.
- Remember, this is a five paragraph theme. Check spelling, run-on sentences, punctuation, and capitalization. Do not label

each paragraph. Write or print legibly in ink, skipping every other line, on one side of your paper only. If using a computer, double-space, indenting paragraphs five spaces. As this is a personal opinion paper, there is no need to use "I" or "I feel" or "I think." *Do not use "I," OK?* Also, do not use words such as "a lot," "good," or "great" to describe the performance. They are too general and basically mean nothing. I want specifics.

- You must consider the reader has not seen the production; consequently, you need to write this paper so the reader can visualize what you saw.

I developed the backstage and acting critiques because it became apparent I needed to give credit to my students who were working crews and/or acting in other productions. We are also a very diverse community, with children's shows and dance concerts, which are certainly valid theatre experiences as subjects for a critique, so I developed critiques for them as well. The Basic Critique Form in the Appendix on page 120 provides information on the various critique formats.

Letter to Parents

```
    I made a big mistake my last semester by not
sending out my parent letter. Wrong-o! I had
calls from disgruntled parents about my subject
matter and/or course management. It had all been
spelled out in my letter I had not sent home.
Dumb me!
```

Before your year gets into full swing, you have one more important thing to do: send a letter home introducing yourself and your course. In this age of computers, the trick is to make it personal. You could even send an email to that effect.

Oh, I know, I know, there are only twenty-four hours in the day and you are only one person, but it is time well spent. I am including my two letters, the beginning drama class (Letter to Drama 1 Parents) and my advanced class (Letter to Drama 2 Parents). See Appendix page 123.

By requiring each student to have a notebook that included my Course Management and Content, Grade Sheet, Productions Around Missoula, and Basic Critique Format, as well as sending a letter home to parents, I had informed everyone what Margaret Johnson's drama department was all about. We could now begin the all-important theatre must: teamwork.

Introduction Activities

One of the things I feel strongly about is, no matter whether you are teaching teenagers or adults, directing a play or being involved in a community theatre production, you need to start out with at least one group activity so everyone can be introduced to one another. We do not get to know people by osmosis. We will be working with each other for the span of six to eight weeks when doing a play or nine to thirty-six weeks when we are teaching. You will only get to know your students better.

```
    It would not be a bad idea to review your
class rules again, even if you are teaching the
same  students,  at  the  beginning  of  a  new
semester  and take time  to play one  of these
games.
```

We all remember those essay assignments "What I Did This Summer" or "What I Did During Christmas Vacation" — boring! They do tell us something about our student's summertime or winter activities and also how they use grammar, but it does not let us know who our students really are.

Yes, I know, you may not be a drama teacher, but you still want to know your students whether you are a language arts teacher in junior high or a senior AP teacher. And yes, we have our subject to teach and need all the time we can to give those students every advantage when it comes to national standards. However, before all learning can take place, our students need to feel comfortable in the classroom and with their fellow students. Building an atmosphere of acceptance and trust is paramount to a successful classroom. When that is accomplished, who knows how much our students can achieve?

The following games, often called icebreakers, are nonthreatening, which is why I found them successful. I did not use all of them every year, but I always started with Picnic.

Picnic

On the first day of school, I played Picnic with all my students, both English and drama. After I had seated them and handed out and discussed my Course Management and Content, I would spend time during the rest of the first week discussing Plays Around Missoula, the Grade Sheet, and the Basic Critique Format. And then we would go on a picnic!

```
Before we started, I would remind them this
was a school-sanctioned activity so they had to
keep that in mind. We needed to stress keeping
context appropriate to the content!
```

The student I selected to begin the game would say his or her first name and then he or she would bring something to the picnic beginning with the letter of their first name. For example, "Hi, my name is Margaret, and I am going to bring mustard." The next student then says, "Hi, this is Margaret, (indicating the first student) and she is bringing mustard. I am Brad, and I'm bringing a basketball."

This would continue until half the class had responded. My classes were small, so I would divide the class in half. We would only do eight to ten students and then we would start over. I felt, as this was the first day of class, I didn't want to overwhelm them with having to remember sixteen to twenty names and items at once. If a student could not remember everyone's name and item, it was fine. I just let the student name those he or she remembered.

When everyone had "taken" something to the picnic, I would ask if anyone would like to say everyone's name and what he or she was bringing. I always had at least two students who could name all the items and most of the names. I would let them go on even if they couldn't remember everyone. Someone always helped them out. Even two weeks after school had started, or even at the end of the year, we would review our picnic and it was amazing how the students remembered!

Sharing

An easy, nonthreatening activity is to divide the class into four groups or four corners of the room using the following designations and have them share something about themselves:

- Birth month *and* their favorite movie:
    January — March
    April — June
    July — September
    October — December
- Favorite season *and* their favorite sport:
    Fall
    Winter
    Spring
    Summer
- First name *and* where it came from:
    A-F
    G-L
    M-R
    S-Z
- First name spelled backwards *and* their favorite toy when they were little:
    A-F
    G-L
    M-R
    S-Z

Introduce Themselves

A fun introduction game is to have your students introduce themselves, but with a twist. In advance, you have prepared two introduction sheets on two different colors of paper. See the examples Introduction Group A and Introduction Group B, in the Appendix on pages 127 and 128. Have on hand a picture frame. I did not have one, so I bought a large framing mat. Pass out the introduction sheets. Be sure half the class has one color and the other half the other color. Give them five minutes to fill out the form. Then have your students pair off, one with each color. Give them three to four minutes to read each other's sheet. The point is they are going to introduce their partner, not themselves. They are only to cover three things on the sheet, plus the person's name. The person being introduced holds the frame in front of his or her face as the partner introduces him or her.

```
You will notice I mentioned giving your
students three to four minutes to prepare.
Throughout the book I will be referring to
various time limits. If you are like me, it is
hard to keep track of time. So, many years ago
I invested in kitchen timers and was always on
the lookout for the newest and brightest! That
way, when I said they had three to four minutes,
I knew indeed they had three to four minutes. I
think it is a great investment, not only in
keeping everyone on track, but being fair to
each group.

I also mention using a 3 x 5 card box to store
cards. This is another invaluable purchase. It
allows you to use and reuse various prompts for
numerous games and activities.

Having a hat or a cup handy, from which to
draw numbers, names, etc., is another must for
your classroom.
```

2 Truths and 1 Lie

If you have a more advanced group, who knows each other very well, instead of the above introductions, you might like to give it another twist with the following introduction game.

Have your class pair off and tell their partner three things about themselves — two that are true and one that is a lie. For example, he or she might tell the partner about his or her hobbies, favorite class, favorite food, family member, or where he or she has travelled. Or he or she might choose to tell three everyday facts or three more unusual things, but remember only one of them should be a lie.

Make sure the partners listen carefully to what he or she has said. Afterwards, the partner tries to guess which was the lie. Have the entire group get into a circle and each pair introduces the partner to the rest of the group with the three facts. Can the group guess which was the lie?

Next, get back into pairs and the other partner will tell the partner things about him or herself that are *all true*. Listen carefully. Now, the whole group makes a circle again and each partner introduces the other partner to the group by telling two of the true things their partner has told them and a lie he or she has made up. See if the group can pick the lie!

Toilet Paper

If your room has space limitations, pass around one roll of toilet paper or pass around two rolls of toilet paper at opposite sides of the class. Tell your students to take enough toilet paper for a weekend camp trip.

After everyone has gotten their pieces of tissue, they are to introduce themselves by using their squares of toilet paper. For each square they have taken, they are to share something about themselves.

Hello

Have your students mill about the room and greet each other, saying their name as they shake hands with everyone else in the room. This continues for several minutes. Then have each student greet each other, as if they were one of the following:

- A Queen or King of England
- A smelly person
- Someone who has just coughed
- Someone who makes you angry
- Someone you are afraid of

- Someone you want to share a secret with
- Your best friend
- Your idol
- Your long lost brother or sister

Thirty Second Handshake

Have everyone walk around the room, shaking hands with everyone else by saying "Hello" and their name — within thirty seconds. As a variation, give a signal for the class to switch between normal and slow motion or slow speech.

Large Group Activities

The following large group activities do not necessarily need to be done the first week but can be done at any time during your semester or school year. This early in the semester or school year you don't want your students to be "put on the spot." Yes, several of the following activities do have one person "on the spot," but he or she is working with the whole group. The difference is the approach.

Clap Hands

Have everyone sit in a circle and number off, starting with one, so everyone has a number. Then you start a rhythm: two claps on the thighs using both hands, two hand claps together, and then two snaps of the fingers. Practice this until everyone can do it. Now comes the tricky part: when the two snaps happen, the person with the number one is to say his or her number on the first snap and another student's number on the second snap. Then everyone claps their thighs, claps their hands together, and when it comes time for the snaps, the person whose number was called says his or her number on the first snap and another number in the circle with the second. The trick is to keep a steady rhythm, not breaking it because someone does not remember his or her number. If they do not notice when their number is called, have the person who said the number start over.

In order to make it a bit more difficult, have the person who messes up become the last number. Of course, many people's numbers then change and the trick is to remember your new number. To make it even more difficult, various rules can be put into effect such as no reverse numbers, no number to the direct right or left of you, etc.

Most Deaths in a Minute

Select ten to twelve students, let them separate into two teams, and line up in front of the class. Choose two students from the audience as counters. The teams compete for the greatest number of deaths they can act out in one minute. Each death must be different and unique. Be creative!

Group Stop

After everyone has quietly walked leisurely around the room, one student will elect to freeze in a position, unexpectedly. As soon as another student notices someone has frozen in position, he or she freezes as well. The effect of one person freezing causes everyone to freeze. Once everyone is frozen, the group starts milling around again. The goal is to see how quickly the group can freeze in position.

To Catch a Thief

After your students have formed a circle and closed their eyes, walk around the circle, and tap one student on the back. I often walked around the circle several times before I selected the specific student. After you have finished walking around the room, say, "Whomever I touched has taken my school keys from my desk drawer. Now open your eyes and everyone look and feel guilty." Then go around the circle asking each student if he or she took the keys. They are all to answer "no." Afterwards, have the group try to guess who stole the keys. You might want to tap several students or none, and see if there is a difference.

Alien, Cow, Tiger

Once again, the class forms a circle. There are three animals a player can be:

- An alien — hold your index fingers up next to your head, as little antennae, and say "bleep bleep," bending towards the center circle.
- A cow — bending forward, holding your right hand on your tummy, say, "moo."
- A tiger — reaching forward with your hands imitating claws and "growl."

Each player decides to become one of the three. *He or she does not share his or her decision.* The ultimate goal is for everyone to become the same. When you say, "go!" everyone is to be what he or she chooses. Redo this until everyone is in sync. Do not spend more than about three minutes on this. Hopefully it is long enough. You might even have the class invent their own animals or things.

```
    In my adult class, I tried this once with
great success; however, I tried it again with
another class and had one obstinate person who
absolutely would not change being a tiger —
everyone had better be a tiger or else! Needless
to say, the game was over in less than three
minutes.
```

Who Started the Motion

This time your students are standing in a circle. Explain that someone is going to be "it," and then send that student out of the room. When that person is gone, someone else volunteers to start a motion. It can be hand clapping, head nodding, winking, bending, and/or any kind of appropriate movement, but no vocal sounds. He or she has to change the movement every thirty seconds. It can be a slight change, going from a big nodding of the head to a smaller nod or a jerkier movement to one much smoother, etc. You may have to coach, giving the volunteer the thirty-second warning.

As soon as the volunteer starts the motion, the entire circle must join in immediately and the "it" person comes back and stands in the middle of the circle.

The goal of the circle is to protect the volunteer by everyone in the circle changing the motion each time the volunteer initiates a change, without looking directly at the volunteer. The "it" person's job is to figure out who the volunteer is. The "it" person will be given three guesses. If he or she figures it out, great, the volunteer becomes "it," going out of the room and another volunteer begins his or her movement, etc. If the "it" person doesn't figure out who the volunteer is after three guesses, the volunteer still becomes "it."

Pass the Tennis Ball

This game sounds easy but actually requires real concentration. Again, you have your class in a circle and ask for a volunteer to be in the middle. Ask the volunteer to close his or her eyes. Pass a tennis ball clockwise around the circle. The reason for having the volunteer's eyes closed is so he or she won't know who has the ball when he or she calls "stop."

When the volunteer calls "stop," the person holding the tennis ball calls out a letter in the alphabet and passes the tennis ball around the circle, while the volunteer has to name six nouns (no proper names, places, or things) starting with that letter. Do not allow the tougher letters, like X, for example.

The goal for the volunteer is to name six nouns before the ball comes back to the person who had the ball when the volunteer said "stop." If the volunteer cannot name six (no help from fellow students), he or she changes places with the person who called out the letter. If the volunteer names six, on the sixth noun, the ball will stop and whoever has the ball becomes the volunteer.

You may have to keep track of all the letters called. You do not want to have a letter called twice. As your students become better players, increase the number of words required.

Improvisation

I loved to start my class doing several easy improvisation games, which can be thought of as "on the spot" or "off the cuff" spontaneous activities, spoken or written, without prior preparation, involving large groups. As well as being wonderful introduction games, they are also great for refocusing a group that has become scattered or one that has become bored!

A Short History of Improvisational Theatre

Before I began any games, I wanted my students to understand something about improvisation. Begin by asking your students what the word *improvisation* means. I started with what they knew, using the simple retelling of a joke, exaggerated, of course, as we do every day. Make sure they realize improvisational games increase creativity, besides being fun to play. Next, give them a short history of improvisational theatre.

The Commedia Dell'Arte

The most direct ancestor of modern improvisation is probably *commedia dell'arte,* which was popular throughout Europe for almost 200 years starting in the mid-1500s. Troupes of performers would travel from town to town, presenting shows in the public squares and on makeshift stages. They would improvise all their dialogue, within an outline provided by a set "scenario." There is more about commedia in Unit 4.

Viola Spolin

In the 1930s, Viola Spolin, a theatre director, began to develop a new approach to directing based on the simple and powerful idea that children and adults would enjoy learning the craft of acting if it were presented as a series of games. "The games emerged out of necessity," she said. "I didn't sit at home and dream them up. When I had a problem [directing], I made up a game. When another problem came up, I just made up a new game." Spolin's son, Paul Sills, built on his mother's work and was one of the driving forces of improvisational theatre in Chicago in the 1950s. He created an ensemble of actors who developed a kind of "modern commedia," which eventually led to the development of a company called Second City. It appeals to the average man in the street, bringing people to the theatre who in many cases had never gone before. Stephen Colbert, Amy Poehler, Steve Carell, and Tina Fey are just a few of its graduates.

Keith Johnstone and Theatresports

Keith Johnstone started formulating his theories about creativity and spontaneity while growing up in England. He felt theatre had become pretentious and wanted to bring theatre to the people who went to sporting and boxing matches, the same audience Shakespeare had written for in his day.

Johnstone decided one approach would be to combine elements of both theatre and sports to form a hybrid called Theatresports. The basic rules of team sports were adapted to the improvisational theatre framework. Teams would compete for points awarded by judges, and audiences would be encouraged to cheer for good scenes and jeer the judges (kill the umpire!). Johnstone's ideas have gone on to influence, directly or indirectly, almost every major improv company.

The Dos and Don'ts of Improvisation

Before beginning any of the following activities, be sure your students understand they are considered games rather than assignments. As with any game there are three basic principles I insisted my students follow:

- No breaking character.
- No saying, "I can't," but rather, "I'll try."
- There is no right or wrong way to play any of these games as long as you follow the techniques I have explained.

There are also rules, as with any game.

First discuss the *dos of improvisation:*

- Take cues from scene partner.
- Be spontaneous.
- Make partner look good.

Next discuss the *don'ts of improvisation:*

- Don't negate. Always answer yes.
- Don't be a ham. This is a dialogue, not a monologue.
- Don't ignore or deny scene partner.
- Don't change the storyline. Always use the words given by your partner. You are not to plot the story in advance.
- Don't respond with a question. Acting is doing, not telling.

A Great Two-Minute Improvisation Game to Start Your Drama Class

On the second or third day of class I introduced the following game, demonstrating the rules and we played it throughout the semester and school year. It was a great way to begin class, allowing you to take roll, get ready for the class, and focus your students on the use of improv.

In advance, make up a list of about fifty brief bits of dialogue, which could be used to start improvised scenes. See below and Improvisation Starters in the Appendix on page 129 for suggestions. Write each on a card and keep them in your 3 x 5 card box so they can be used over and over.

Dialogue suggestions:

What's in the box? A puppy?

It's snowing! Let's go sledding.

You're late. I will have to tell Dad.
How's your brother?
Owwww! That hurts. Stop it!
Go away. I'm tired.
It's dark in here. I'm scared.
Here's a dime. Go buy some candy.
Don't forget, it's my birthday.
I'm lost. Help me.
I dare you! I double dare you!

Demonstrate the don'ts. Select one student to read a card to you and you negate. The students will immediately see that the story goes nowhere. If you need to demonstrate the dos, select another student and proceed.

Begin the Game

Depending on the class and your timeframe, you can go around the room and have every student either read a card or react so everyone gets a chance to "play." Then explain to them, starting tomorrow when the bell rings, one student — you decide where to start in the class, usually based on the seating chart — will pick a card and the student seated next to the reader will react. They are to keep the scene going for two minutes allowing you to take roll and get ready for the rest of the class period. Usually, during the first couple of weeks, your students are much more comfortable sitting at their desks, but if you prefer, they can get up in front of the class and perform their improvisation.

Add a New Element

After several weeks, add a new component, which gets your students up out of their seats. Start by setting up a simple playing area in the front of the room. Put two chairs side by side in the playing area. The first actor will sit in a chair and perform some activity in pantomime, like reading a book, feeding birds, etc. The second actor will enter and start the improvisation by using one of the short openers.

I have recently returned to the classroom teaching the over fifty crowd at the University of Montana's School of Extended & Lifelong Learning MOLLI program, using many of the activities I am describing in this unit. Everyone needs to feel comfortable before they embark on "acting." I used these opening cards every time my class met.

One of my students was a wonderful older lady from Sweden who had a great sense of humor and fun. My students and I always looked forward to her contributions to the class. When her partner read to her, "He's dead," she replied without hesitation, "I know. I shot him!" It brought the class to a standstill with laughter and clapping. Of course, there was nowhere to go and the improv ended!

Kindergarten Class

Select twelve actors. Eleven will be kindergarteners and one will be the teacher, who is telling the story of *Goldilocks and the Three Bears*. The actors maintain their characters throughout the scene.

Character and Objective

1. Teacher (M or F): to have students sit quietly and listen to the story
2. Child A (F): to make the teacher comment on what a polite child she is
3. Child B (M): to get the teacher to let him go to the restroom
4. Child C (M or F): to listen to the story
5. Child D (M or F): to be helpful to the teacher
6. Child E (M): to play with the car in his pocket
7. Child F (M or F): to sit close to and get the attention of child A
8. Child G (M): to get child E in trouble without getting in trouble himself
9. Child H (M or F): to get child C to look at him or her

10. Child I (F): to give a piece of candy to child D in order to make child D like her

11. Child J (M or F): to get a piece of candy from child I

12. Child K (F): to show children F and H pictures of her puppy

You will need a chair for the actor who plays the teacher and eleven nametags for the students. The children will sit on the floor. Either take the group of children out of the room and whisper privately to each actor his or her character and objective or have the students select a card with the written information you prepared ahead of time and put in your 3 x 5 card file box. *They are not to share the information with their fellow actors.* Their objectives will become obvious by the way they act.

Just before starting the scene, send the teacher and those who are the audience out of the room. Address the actors playing the children as follows:

"One last point: you are all frightened of the school principal because he is very tall and has a deep voice. None of you want to be sent to the office under any circumstances. Play your objectives carefully because you don't want to cause the teacher to send you to the office. If the teacher tells you to go to the office, you must leave the scene and stand outside in the hall until the improvisation is over."

Next, go outside, send the audience back into the classroom, and speak to the actor portraying the teacher:

"The children are all frightened of the principal. They do not want to be sent to the office. If a child provokes you, you may threaten to send him or her to the office. You don't really want to send anyone there. But, if necessary, you may do so. When you tell a child to go to the office, the actor will leave the scene."

Seat the children on the floor around the teacher to begin the scene. During the improvisation you may want to call on a student from the audience to enter the scene as the principal. This actor has a message for the teacher and could then ask about the behavior of the students. Freeze the scene for discussion if the actors overreact at any time, especially to the entrance of the principal. Call "places" to initiate the improvisation and "curtain" to end it.

Following the improvisation, you may want to have the actors describe how they felt during the scene and how the audience felt by asking these questions:

- Were the actors playing children able to draw on their own memories to help them interpret the roles accurately and honestly?
- Did the actors actually feel the experience of being a kindergartener in class? Or were they acting throughout the scene?
- Did the actor playing the teacher experience any genuine emotions during the scene? What were these emotions?
- What actions on the part of the teacher or the children seemed realistic and believable?
- What was each actor's objective?

Trip to New York

Set up chairs to suggest a bus. Place a desk in one corner for the ticket seller. Choose twelve students who will be taking the bus. They are to create an improvisation based on a character and an objective you will give them. See the example below.

Either take the group out of the room and whisper privately to each actor his or her character and objective or have them select a card with the written information you have prepared ahead of time and put in your card file box. *They are not to share the information with their fellow actors.* By the way they create their characters, their objectives should become obvious.

Character and Objective

1. Teenage girl: to meet her boyfriend, who her parents do not like
2. A cool guy: to make people think he's a rich Yankee fan whose flight to NY was canceled
3. A nervous woman: to meet her online boyfriend for the first time and is embarrassed to tell anyone
4. A middle-aged person (M or F): to be a stage actor in NY
5. An old person (M or F): to visit his or her favorite grandchildren
6. A weird person (M or F): to convince people the end of the world is near
7. An upset man: to return home without the job he was counting on
8. A young person (M or F): to audition for Juilliard
9. A nervous person (M or F): to skip town before he or she is arrested

10. An odd person (M or F): to go to the Cordon Bleu School to become a world-renowned pastry chef
11. Undercover agent (M or F): to identify and arrest a suspect
12. Eight-year-old person (M or F): to wait for his or her mother, who never arrives

All the characters are waiting to get on the bus going to New York except for characters 11 and 12. However, 11 must buy a ticket to protect his or her cover. The actors must maintain their character and objective throughout the scene.

Next determine their order of entry into the scene. Select two more students in the class to be part of the scene, one as a ticket seller (objective: to sell tickets) and one as a security guard (objective: to maintain law and order). The scene should not end until you stop it. Your actors must avoid any action, which might force an early conclusion such as a bomb, the bus driver having a heart attack, or bus failure.

Before you begin the scene, urge your actors to concentrate on their objectives, playing them as realistically as possible, no stereotypes. The scene opens with the ticket seller, security guard, and number 12 seated on a chair waiting for his or her parent. Call "places" to initiate the improvisation and "curtain" to end it.

Following the improvisation, let the audience share what they observed about the actors' characters and motives. Use the questions you asked after the Kindergarten Class improv.

Next, the actors need to state their characters and their individual objectives, as well as any approaches they used to achieve their objective. If the audience does not understand the character or objective, discuss ways the scene or actor could have improved.

```
    In any of these improvisations, be alert for
overacting   or   lack   of   concentration.   If
necessary, freeze the action to call attention
to   such   faults.   This   type   of   large   group
improvisation   can   be   a   marvelous   success,   a
dismal   failure,   or   any   number   of   things   in
between.  Allow  a  good  scene  to  run  no  longer
than  ten  minutes.  A  poor  scene  should  be  cut
short.
```

Students Creating Their Own Large Group Improvisation

Now give your students the opportunity to create their own large group improvisation. This will take several days, depending on your class' ability.

Divide the class into two or three groups of eight to ten students, depending upon class size. Have each group prepare an improvisation in which every member must portray a character with an objective. Instruct each group to decide first on a suitable location for its scene. Then they should come up with characters who fit into that locale.

If any group has trouble thinking of a suitable setting, you will need to be ready with suggestions. The following settings can easily accommodate large groups.

- Beach: An easy scene to develop; actors enter one at a time, starting with the lifeguard.
- Courtroom: Lots of character possibilities; judge, defendant, prosecutor, defense attorney, bailiff, clerk or recorder, witnesses. The group can even select a jury from the rest of the class.
- Funeral parlor: Begin with the director of the establishment alone with the deceased. Have the other actors enter one at a time or in pairs.
- Murder scene: Living room of an old mansion; ten suspects and a detective á la Agatha Christie.
- Play rehearsal: This would depend on whether your students have had prior theatre involvement and have some firsthand experience of play rehearsals to draw from.
- School bus: Driver and any number of students; all kinds of opportunities for interesting interplay of characters and objectives.
- Wedding reception: A difficult and challenging scene; clear-cut relationships must be established beforehand.

Once the scene and characters have been determined, select a group leader who will coordinate casting and help the actors choose characters and their objectives. The leader makes sure there are conflicts, which must be resolved, and then decides in what order the actors are to enter into the scene. Each actor writes down his or her character's name and objective, which is then put in a hat. When the improv is over, each objective is revealed to the audience.

Evaluation

As these are games and improvisations using large groups, a blanket and/or a participation grade can be given. If you want to have individual grades in the improvisations, focus your evaluation on characterization and use of objectives.

Unit 2
Technical Theatre

Why Technical Theatre?

One unit that should be covered in the basic drama class deals with technical theatre. It introduces theatre lingo, the principles of costume, makeup, scenery, lighting, props, and set, as well as important theatre terms needed in maintaining a theatre facility and mounting a successful stage production. As my theatre had no shop, an extremely limited backstage area, and one classroom, which doubled as an English classroom, I lacked proper facilities to teach a hands-on technical unit. I also had a time constraint, as our basic drama class was just a semester long and most students who took the course were interested in acting. I did, however, feel a fundamental knowledge of technical terms was absolutely necessary, as was an understanding of the three basic types of theatre and various areas of theatre production. How else could they write a knowledgeable critique or understand that theatre was not just performing?

In order to be successful with this unit, you need to familiarize yourself with the terms and concepts in order to explain them to your students. If you do not have any technical background, the Internet is a useful place to start. There is no substitute, however, for taking additional classes at a university or college.

Use of Class Time

I spent approximately four weeks on the technical theatre unit, interspersing it with two other units, choral reading and pantomime. I felt committing four straight weeks to tech was too much, too dry. My students wanted to be active. I used a portion of each class period on the technical unit — typically ten minutes or longer, depending on how much time the specific class needed to understand the definitions and concepts.

Evaluation

As technical theatre dealt with definitions and concepts, it was easy to evaluate and these were the only written tests I gave all semester. I created two packets, one on Tech Terms and the other on

Important Areas of Theatre Production on pages 130 and 137 of the Appendix. I felt these terms and concepts were important. By no means did I cover everything, but I wanted my students to have a foundation on which to base their critiques; not that they liked or disliked something, but that they were able to view a play appreciating and enjoying what the director, technicians, and the actors had accomplished.

A Fun Pretest

A great way to start this unit is to give a pretest. Pick ten to twenty terms and ask your students to define them. This will show you how much they know or don't about theatre and it can be fun to see what they think the terms mean.

First Eight Days

I started with the Tech Terms packet dividing it into eight class periods. Each day my students were to review a certain number of terms, their definitions, and come to class with any questions about the terms they reviewed. Sometimes there were very few questions and the majority of the class time was devoted to one of the other units. At other times, there were many questions and half the class time was spent answering their questions. I often gave them a pop quiz on terms we had discussed earlier just so they would realize I was serious about their knowledge of the terms.

After we had covered all the terms, I gave them an extra day to ask any and all questions over anything they missed or were still confused about. You could play the following game as a review for one or both packets. Then I gave them the Technical Terms Final Test on page 147 of the Appendix. I have also included make up tests over both units as there was at least one student who couldn't or didn't attend class the day of the final. The Make Up Test over Technical Terms is on page 149 of the Appendix.

Jeopardy, Theatre Style

Sometimes, instead of an open-ended question and answer review, we played a game loosely based on *Jeopardy* for extra credit points using answers referring to the technical terms and areas of theatre production.

Each student was responsible for a certain number of words or concepts. On the review day, they came to class with the definition of the terms or concepts written out on separate pieces of paper. All the answers were put in a hat. If a student did not come to class prepared, they could not participate, which of course had been explained earlier.

The class was divided into two teams. Each team decided in what order each contestant would answer. Then we decided which team would go first, usually guessing a number I selected and the closest team to that number would start.

Each contestant got only one chance to answer, just like *Jeopardy*. You will need a timer that can count seconds as you give each contestant eight seconds to give "the question." If the contestant does not answer or gives an incorrect "question" within the eight seconds, the "answer" goes to the other team. You keep going until the correct "question" is given. The team who didn't receive the "answer" in the previous round then starts with a new "answer." A point is awarded to each team who answers correctly.

What was the incentive? It could be anything you think is fair. I chose to give the winning team two wrong answers on the test and not be penalized; the losing team would get one wrong answer. It was a bit of a pain to correct, but they had a great time learning and remembering the terms — what I had wanted in the first place. I did not tell them their "prize for winning" until the game was over to maintain suspense.

Second Eight Days

Just as I did with the tech terms, I divided the Important Areas of Theatre Production packet into eight class period discussions.

```
    As  I  was  not  particularly  adept  at
demonstrating makeup, I invested in a makeup
video when I was talking about makeup. Videos
are available from most play publishers.
Meriwether Publishing has several very good
ones. Today there are stage makeup demos
available on the Internet and YouTube.
```

Students could again ask any questions over their readings they did not understand, taking as much time as needed to cover the information. If I were in production, I would tell them the specifics about that production.

When the eight days were up, I again gave them a review day or played a second *Jeopardy* game. The following day, I gave the Theatre Production Test on page 151 of the Appendix. I have also included the Make Up Test over Theatre Production on page 153 of the Appendix.

Opportunity to Do Tech Theatre?

A question I am sure you are asking is how did my students get real life experience with technical theatre? As we did at least two major productions a year, those students interested had ample opportunity to become involved with most technical areas. Due to safety, my students did not focus lights or get on high ladders when working on sets. Often I would hire a coordinator to spearhead work on lights, set, and costumes. The coordinator involved the students as much as they wanted to be involved. My students always handled props, makeup, and publicity.

For my advanced drama classes, all the students were involved not only onstage, but backstage as well. They designed and executed sets (no high ladders), costumes, props, lights (except focusing), and publicity.

Unit 3
Choral Reading

Why Choral Reading?

Acting requires the use of expression both vocally and physically to create the characters in any given play or monologue. I always began with choral reading, a great way to start students learning to appreciate their own vocal abilities. So what is choral reading? An interpretive reading of a text, often poetry, rhymes, tongue twisters, or songs, by a group (chorus) of voices speaking in unison, generally without solos or very few under the direction of a leader or teacher. The key words here are *group* and *reading*. Reading and/or acting alone with a memorized piece in front of a group, especially early in the year, can cause performance anxiety among many of your students. By doing group readings, rather than solo presentations, your students are:

- Gaining practice of performing.
- Using expression to convey an author's intent.
- Beginning to realize how their vocal interpretation can enhance the meaning of the printed word.
- Learning how important their vocal instrument is in creating a character.

All of this can be accomplished without your students feeling anxious or embarrassed.

A Very Short History

Choral reading began in ancient Greece with lyric poetry (poetry written to music). It was originally performed at religious festivals in honor of Dionysus, the god of the grape harvest and winemaking. These festivals were comprised of large groups of people speaking in unison (chorus), under the direction of a leader. These religious festivals evolved into competitive drama festivals, changing the storyline to include narration of local battles and heroes. Each town had its own chorus, which competed for prizes.

In 534 B.C., theatre was born when Thespis, a Greek poet, stepped out from the chorus, becoming the first character to exchange words with the leader of the chorus. This conversation became dialogue. The term *thespian* is synonymous with actor, in his honor.

So How Do We Start?

Though enjoyable, reading aloud effectively and fluently takes skill and practice. Explain to your students that they must first know what they are reading, because their presentation adds to the understanding and meaning of the piece. They need to be very familiar with every aspect of the piece; therefore, choral reading requires repeated practice readings, one of the reasons to choose *short* texts like poetry, rhymes, tongue twisters, or songs. It is better to start out with shorter pieces because they are easier to learn and do successfully. Of course, if you want to present a long piece you certainly can.

You want your first piece to have:

* Passages with interesting sounds.
* Contrasts that can be interpreted by volume, inflection, dialogue.
* Changes in mood.
* Sounds such as clapping or singing to make the passage more dramatic.

You want your students to make the words come alive. The easiest way of doing this is incorporating some of the following techniques:

* Alternating slow and fast lines, stanzas, and paragraphs.
* Alternating loud and soft phrases and lines.
* Alternating high and low voices — possibly male and female.
* Emphasizing key words and phrases.

By having the entire class working as one group, with you as the leader, helps set the pace as well as modeling proper pronunciation, rhythm, and expression. You will also be introducing them to the following terms and techniques, helping to divide up the piece and giving it life.

* CHO: The teacher and the class read the poem together. It is important to remember when speaking with one voice there must be clear enunciation as well as a blending of the voices. You must sound like one voice. No voice should stick out. It is exactly like singing in a choir.

- CHO 1, 2, etc.: Two or more smaller groups take turns reading different parts of the poem.
- One line per reader: Each reader is given a line or two to read.
- With an echo: One person reads a line or phrase and the group repeats or echoes it.
- Adding on: One person or group starts reading, and another person or group joins in with each new line or section.
- Expression: Personal feeling and emotion expressed in the reading of a piece.
- Rhythm: Ease with which a poem is read and the flow of rising and falling sounds.
- Slash: (/) Means pause or break.

I have chosen two pieces, "The Daniel Jazz" by Vachel Lindsay and "George" by Hilaire Belloc, as good beginning pieces. See below:

"The Daniel Jazz"

by Vachel Lindsay

Note: This poem has a certain beat to it. Don't let it drag. My notes on performance are in parentheses.

CHO: Darius the Mede was a king and a wonder.
    His eye was proud, and his voice was thunder.
    Brrrrupppp ... boom *(Very loud)*
    He kept bad lions in a monstrous den.
    He fed up *(Raise voice up on the word "up")* the lions on Christian men. *(Voice goes down on "men")*.
    Daniel was chief hired man of the land.
    He stirred up the Jazz of the palace band.
    He stirred up the Jazz of the / palace band.
    (Sing the first two phrases of "Alexander's Rag Time Band" using the word "dud.")
    He white washed the cellar.
    He shoveled in the coal.
    And Daniel kept a-praying:
DAN: "Lord save my soul."
CHO: Daniel kept a-praying;
DAN: "Lord save my soul."

CHO: Daniel was the butler, swagger and swell.
    He ran upstairs. He answered the bell.
GIRLS: BRINGGGG.
DAN: "Old man Ahab leaves his card.
    Elisha and the bears are a-waiting in the yard.
    Here comes Pharaoh and his snakes a-calling.
    Shadrach, Meshach, and Abednego for tea.
    And Jonah and the whale
    And the sea!
CHO: Wheeee!
DAN: Here comes St. Peter and his fishing pole.
    Here comes Judas and his silver a-calling."
CHO: And Daniel kept a-praying: *(Each one of these gets louder)*
DAN: "Lord save my soul."
CHO: Daniel kept a-praying
DAN: "Lord save my soul."
CHO: Daniel kept a-praying
DAN: "Lord save my soul."
GIRLS: *(So sweet, soft, and a bit high)* His sweetheart and his mother were
    Christian and meek.
    They washed and ironed for
    Darius every week.
CHO: *(Use a very deep voice — nasty type, very staccato)*
    One Thursday he met them at the door:
    Paid them, as usual, but acted sore.
    He said:
DAN: *(Nasty — dastardly)* "Your Daniel is a dead little pigeon.
    He's a good hard worker, but he talks religion."
CHO: And he showed them Daniel in the lion's cage.
    Daniel is standing quietly, the lions in a rage. *(Roar!)*
CHO: His good mother cried:
GIRL: *(High voice with lots of breath)* "Lord save him,
    Send Gabriel. Send Gabriel."
CHO: King Darius said to the lions:
DAR: *(Nasty — dastardly)* "Bite Daniel. Bite Daniel.

Bite him. Bite him. Bite him."
CHO: Thus roared the lions:
BOYS: "We want Daniel, Daniel, Daniel
   (Very loud) Grrrr
   (Much louder than the first time) We want Daniel, Daniel,
   Daniel.
   Yummmm.
CHO: *(Very calm)* And Daniel did not frown,
   Daniel did not cry.
   He kept looking at the sky.
   And the Lord said to Gabriel:
BOYS: *(Monotone/chant but get louder and louder and the last
   line—very fast)*
   "Go chain the lions down,
   Go chain the lions down.
   Go chain the lions down."
CHO: And Gabriel chained the lions,
   And Gabriel chained the lions,
   And Gabriel chained the lions,
CHO: And Daniel got out of the den,
DAN: "I is a getting out of here."
CHO: And Daniel got out of the den,
DAN: "I is a getting out of here."
CHO: And Daniel got out of the den,
DAN: "I is free."
CHO: And Darius said
DAR: "You're a Christian child,"
CHO: And Darius said
DAR: "You're a Christian child,"
CHO: And Darius said
DAR: "You're a Christian child,"
CHO: And gave him back his job again,
   And gave him back his job again,
   And gave him back his job again. *(Again, sing the first two
   phrases of "Alexander's Rag Time Band" using the word
   "dud.")*
   HALLELUJAH *(very loud and happy, stressing all the
   syllables!)*

George

By Hilaire Belloc

Note: This piece has natural builds and pacing and requires vocal characters when introducing the "injured." My notes on performance are in parentheses.

CHO: *(Very upper crust/English)* When George's Grand mamma was told

1: That George had been as good as gold,

CHO: She promised in the afternoon

2: To buy him an Immense *(Make this word as loud as its meaning) Balloon.*

CHO: And so she did / but when it came,

3: *(Do some foreshadowing, make it ominous)* It got into the candle flame,

4: And being of a dangerous sort

CHO: Exploded *(Drag out all three syllables)* with a loud report *(Say "re-port ta." As each of these is spoken each gets louder and faster until the word "crashed," draw it out as well, "ka-rashed-ed-ed-ed")*

5: The lights went out!

6: The windows broke!

7: The room was filled with reeking smoke

8: And in the darkness shrieks and yells

9: Were mingled with electric bells,

10: And fallen masonry and groans,

11: And crunching, as of broken bones,

12: And dreadful shrieks, when, worst of all,

CHO: The house itself began to fall!

13: It *(Stutter this as if it is falling)* tottered, shuddering to and fro,

CHO: Then crashed into the street below.

14: *(There is no feeling in this line, just upper crust!)* Which happened to be Seville Row.

****

GIRLS: *(Out of breath)* When help arrived, among the injured were *(Create voices for each of these people — make it fun.)*

15: Cousin Mary,
16: Little Fred,
17: The Footmen (both of them),
18: The Groom,
19: The man that cleaned the Billiard-Room,
20: The chaplain, and
21: The Still-Room maid.
BOYS: And we are dreadfully afraid
That Monsieur Champignon, the Chief,
22: Will now be
CHO: *(Scream this)* Permanently deaf —
23: And both his aids are much the same;
CHO: While George,
24: Who was in part to blame,
25: Received,
BOYS: You will regret to hear,
GIRLS: A nasty lump behind the ear.
CHO: The moral is
BOYS: That little boys should not be given dangerous toys.

Working With Smaller Groups

After you have shared several pieces with your class as a whole, you will want to divide your class into three groups and give each group a tongue twister. This offers genuine opportunity for problem solving, as each group works out its own presentation. The enjoyment and learning comes out of the process of figuring out *how* to perform the tongue twister, rather than the performance itself. Tell your students the object is to speak in one voice, as fast and interesting as possible. *There are to be no solos in the exercise.* Below are the three I used.

Tongue Twister 1

I bought a batch of baking powder and baked a batch of biscuits.
I brought a big basket of biscuits back to the bakery
and baked a basket of big biscuits.
Then I took the big basket of biscuits
and the basket of big biscuits
and mixed the big baskets

with the basket of biscuits
that was next to the big basket
and put a bunch of biscuits
from the baskets into a box.
Then I took the box of mixed biscuits
and a biscuit mixer and the biscuit basket
and brought the basket of biscuits
and the box of mixed biscuits
and the biscuit mixer
back to the bakery and opened up a can of sardines.

Tongue Twister 2.

Betty Botta bought some butter
"But," said she, "this butter's bitter,
If I put it in my batter,
It will make my batter bitter.
But a bit of better butter,
Will make my bitter batter better."
So, she bought a bit of butter,
Better than the bitter butter,
And it made her bitter batter better.
So 'twas better Betty Botta bought
A bit of better butter.

Tongue Twister 3.

Theophilus Thistle, the successful Thistle sifter,
in sifting a sieve full of unsifted thistles,
thrust three thousand thistles through the thick of his thumb.
Now, if Theophilus Thistle,
the successful thistle sifter,
in sifting a sieve full of unsifted thistles,
thrust three thousand thistles through the thick of his thumb,
see that thou in sifting a sieve full of unsifted thistles,
thrust not three thousand thistles
through the thick of my thumb.
Success to the successful thistle sifter.

Jabberwocky

After you have done the above tongue twisters, a great piece to have your students work on is "Jabberwocky." With all the nonsense words and the hint of action required to read it, your class will have a great time first figuring out what the words might mean, and then using their vocal skills to convey the meaning of the poem. Remind them that pauses might be helpful, as well as interesting vocal sounds. Divide your class into six groups and give them about twenty minutes to prepare their version of this poem.

Jabberwocky

By Lewis Carroll

GROUP 1:
'Twas brillig, and the slithy toves
Did gyre and gimble in the wabe;
All mimsy were the borogoves,
And the mome raths outgrabe.

GROUP 2:
"Beware the Jabberwock, my son!
The jaws that bite, the claws that catch!
Beware the Jubjub bird, and shun
The frumious Bandersnatch!"

GROUP 3:
He took his vorpal sword in hand;
Long time the manxome foe he sought —
So rested he by the Tumtum tree,
And stood awhile in thought.

GROUP 4:
And, as in uffish thought he stood,
The Jabberwock, with eyes of flame,
Came wiffling through the tulgey wood,
And burbled as it came!

GROUP 5:
One, two! One, two! And through and through
The vorpal blade went snicker-snack!
He left it dead, and with its head
He went galumphing back.

GROUP 6:
"And, hast thou slain the Jabberwock?
Come to my arms, my beamish boy!
O frabjous day! Callooh! Callay!"
He chortled in his joy.

GROUP 1:
'Twas brillig, and the slithy toves
Did gyre and gimble in the wabe;
All mimsy were the borogoves,
And the mome raths outgrabe.

Halloween

Sometimes it is fun to take part of a class period, during a particular season, and devote the time to celebrating that season. Below are three rather gruesome poems that my students, especially the boys, loved to do around Halloween. They are taken from Jack Prelutsky's book, *Nightmares: Poems to Trouble Your Sleep*. These may not be appropriate for every school or classroom, so make sure that they are suitable for your school district and community.

Divide the class into three groups, making sure you have boys in each group. Remind them again to make use of sounds. "Crunching" is a great example. What can be done with this word? It can be divided into three syllables, the first sounding like a growl and ending as you did with "Exploded with a loud report" in "George." The author has wonderful words that lend themselves to explosive sounds. Enjoy!

The Ghoul

The gruesome ghoul, the grisly ghoul,
without the slightest noise
waits patiently beside the school
to feast on girls and boys.
He lunges fiercely through the air
as they come out to play,
then grabs a couple by the hair
and drags them far away.
He cracks their bones and snaps their backs
and squeezes out their lungs,
he chews their thumbs like candy snacks
and pulls apart their tongues.
He slices their stomachs and bites their hearts
and tears their flesh to shreds,
he swallows their toes like toasted tarts
and gobbles down their heads.
Fingers, elbows, hands and knees
and arms and legs and feet —
he eats them with delight and ease,
for every part's a treat.
And when the gruesome, grisly ghoul
has nothing left to chew,
he hurries to another school
and waits ... perhaps for you. [1]

The Troll

Be wary of the loathsome troll
that slyly lies in wait
to drag you to his dingy hole
and put you on his plate.
His blood is black and boiling hot,
he gurgles ghastly groans.
He'll cook you in his dinner pot,

---

1 Poem from *Nightmares* © 1976 Jack Prelutsky. Used by permission of HarperCollins Publishers.

your skin, your flesh, your bones.
He'll catch your arms and clutch your legs
and grind you to a pulp,
then swallow you like scrambled eggs —
gobble! gobble! gulp!
So watch your steps when next you go
upon a pleasant stroll,
or you might end in the pit below
as supper for the troll. [2]

The Ogre

In a foul and filthy cavern
where the sun has never shone,
the one-eyed ogre calmly gnaws
a cold and moldy bone.
He sits in silence in the slime
that fills his fetid home
and notes the nearing footsteps
in the monstrous catacomb.
The one-eyed ogre drools with joy,
his stony heart beats fast,
he knows that for some girl or boy
this day shall be their last.
He wields his ugly cudgel
in a wide and vicious arc,
it swiftly finds his victim
in the deep and deadly dark.
Then down and down and down again
the ogre's blows descend,
to rend, and render senseless,
to speed his victim's end.
So pity those who stumble through
the one-eyed ogre's cave —
that dark abode he calls his home
shall surely be their grave. [3]

2, 3 Poems from *Nightmares* © 1976 Jack Prelutsky. Used by permission of HarperCollins Publishers.

Evaluation

If you feel the tongue twisters and "Jabberwocky" should be graded, give them a participation grade. For any other choral readings, divide your class into three or four groups, depending on your class size. As this is a group-oriented unit, each group will work on a piece you have selected, stressing the fact they have to work as a group, because they will be graded as a group. Yes, they can have solos, but the primary goal is group work. Each group has to again figure out *how* to perform their piece, keeping in mind they have to first understand the meaning of the piece, and then add the various techniques we had worked on with "The Daniel Jazz" and "George" to help tell the story. Three more choral pieces, "A Man Named Hods," "The Pobble Who Has No Toes," and "Don't Ever Seize a Weasel by the Tail" can be found in the Appendix on pages 155, 156, and 157. You could also have an additional set of tongue twisters with different groups performing them for another group grade.

Anguish Languish

What the heck is "anguish languish"? It is a form of a *malapropism,* a mistaken use of a word in place of a similar sounding one. An unbelievable number of English words, regardless of their usual meanings, can be substituted quite satisfactorily for others. When all the words in a given passage have been replaced, the passage keeps its original meaning. Remember when this unit was first introduced, I mentioned that your students must first know what they are reading, because their presentation adds to the understanding and meaning of the piece? The real trick with the following piece is to really make sure your students understand what they are reading. Then the audience will know what the "new" words mean and be able to follow the story enjoying the misuse of vocabulary.

I often used the following piece with my advanced students. That is not to say it couldn't be used with beginners. My students loved it. Arthur Godfrey first read "Ladle Rat Rotten Hut" in the 1950s. This piece has also been used as a humorous solo at speech contests. It does take lots of practice, but worth every minute!

Ladle Rat Rotten Hut (Little Red Riding Hood)

By Howard L. Chace

Note: For the first few lines I've given the "translation" in parentheses to help you get started.

CHO: Wants pawn term dare worsted ladle gull hoe lift wetter
(Once upon a time there was a little girl who lived with her)
murder inner ladle cordage honor itch offer lodge, dock, florist.
(mother in a little cottage on the edge of a dark forest.)
CHO 1: Disk ladle gull orphan worry putty ladle rat cluck wetter
ladle rat hut, and fur disk
(This little girl often wore a little red cloak with a pretty little red hat and for this)
raisin pimple colder Ladle Rat Rotten Hut.
(reason people called her Little Red Riding Hood)
CHO: Wan moaning
    1: rat rotten hut's
    2: murder colder inset:
"Ladle rat rotten hut, heresy ladle basking winsome burden barter and shirker cockles. Tick disc ladle basking to dor cordage ofhzr gioin murder hoe lets honor udder she onbr florist. Shaker lake, dun stopper laundry wrote, end yonder nor sorghum stenches dun stopper torque wet strainers."
    1: "Hoe-cake, murder,"
CHO 2: resplendent
    1: ladle rat rotten hut,
CHO 2: end tickle ladle basking an stuttered oft.
CHO 1: Honor wrote tudor cordage offer groin murder,
    1: ladle rat rotten hut
CHO 1: mitten anomalous woof.
    3: "Wail, wail, wail,"
CHO: set disc wicket woof,
    3: "evanescent ladle rat rotten hut! Wares or putty ladle gull goring wizard ladle basking?"
    1: "Armor goring tumor groin murder's,"
CHO: represal ladle gull.
    1: "Grammars seeking bet. Armor ticking arson burden barter

end shirker cockles."

    3: "O hoe! Heifer blessing woke,"

CHO 2: setter wicket woof, butter taught tomb shelf,

    3: "Oil tickle shirt court tudor cordage offer groin murder. Oil ketchup wetter letter, an den - O bore!"

CHO: Soda wicket woof tucker shirt court,

CHO 1: end whinney retched a cordage offer groin murder, picket inner widow

CHO 2: an sore debtor pore oil worming worse lion inner bet.

CHO: Inner flesh disc abdominal woof lipped honor betting adder rope. Zany pool dawn a groin murder's nut cup an gnat gun, any curdle dope inner bet.

CHO 1 : Inner ladle wile

    1: ladle rat rotten hut

CHO 1: a raft attar cordage an ranker dough bell.

    3: "Comb ink, sweat hard,"

CHO: setter wicket woof, disgracing is verse.

    1: Ladle rat rotten hut

CHO: entity bet rum end stud buyer groin murder's bet.

    1: "Oh grammar,"

CHO: crater ladle gull,

    1: "Wart bag icer gut! A nervous sausage bag ice!"

    3: "Buttered lucky chew whiff, doling,"

CHO: whiskered disc ratchet woof wetter wicket small.

    1: "Oh grammar, water bag noise! A nervous sore suture anonialous prognosis!"

    3: "Buttered small your whiff,"

CHO: inserter woof, ants mouse worse waddling.

    1: "Oh grammar, water bag mousey gut! A nervous sore suture bag mouse!"

CHO 2: Daze worry on forger nut gull's lest warts.

CHO: Oil offer sodden

CHO 1: throne offer carvers and sprinkling otter bet,

CHO: disc curl and bloat Thursday woof

CHO 1: ceased pore ladle rat rotten hut an garbled erupt.

CHO: Mural: Yonder nor sorghum stenches shut ladle gulls stopper torque wet strainers.

Two More Choral Reading Activities and Evaluation

Below are two more activities that work well, if you want to extend this unit.

Using a Children's Book or Nursery Rhyme

Divide the class into three or four groups, each selecting a favorite children's book or nursery rhyme. Have them work together to either use the piece itself or write a choral poem, expressing the different points of view of the characters in the piece. Make sure they think about the characters' feelings, voices, and the terms mentioned above.

Using a Novel, Current Event, or Subject

In groups of four, select a current event, novel, or subject and work together to compose an original choral poem. Each voice in the poem should express a side of the argument or controversy. For example, if the subject is curfew, write about the pros and cons of a curfew. One student might read the voice of the parent, another might be a different parent with an opposing point of view, while another might be the voice of their child. Your students should use what they have learned about expression, fluency, and rhythm to compose and present their poem.

Some Great Resources

Below is a list of authors and/or pieces that would make great choral readings:

- Archie Campbell's "Rindercella" (can also be found on YouTube)
- John Ciardi's "I Wouldn't"
- E.E. Cummings' "in Just – "
- T.S. Eliot's *Old Possum's Book of Practical Cats* including "Macavity: The Mystery Cat" and "Gus: The Theatre Cat"
- Walt Kelly's "Pogo" (can also be found on YouTube)
- Ogden Nash's "The Boy Who Laughed at Santa Claus"
- Edgar Allan Poe's "The Raven"
- Anything by Dr. Seuss
- Nancy Shaw's "Sheep in a Jeep," "Sheep in a Shop," "Sheep Take a Hike," etc.

- Shel Silverstein's *A Giraffe and a Half*
- Roald Dahl's "The Tummy Beast"
- James Thurber's Fables including "The Little Girl and the Wolf," "The Last Flower," and "The Unicorn in the Garden"
- Dean Walley's *Puck's Peculiar Pet Shop*
- Any other poems by Jack Prelutsky

Unit 4
Mime

Why Mime?

Now that your students have explored their vocal abilities, they need to begin using physical movement to express themselves. There will be times when an actor doesn't have anything to say verbally, but he or she needs to be able to communicate and react without speaking. Mime is an excellent way to introduce movement. It does not use voice, props, or scenery. Your students can create the illusion of any character, location, object, weather condition, and mood by using their entire body, including the face. Mime allows your students the freedom to climb Mount Everest or take a stroll down a Paris street, to run from a monster, or take a ride in a taxi. Think of mime as the freedom to be able to go anywhere your students' imaginations can take them.

The two words pantomime and mime cause quite a problem for those who try to explain them. While some feel pantomime alludes to a performance, others think mime represents the performer. There are many theories. For the most part, the words are now interchangeable. I will be using both terms.

I felt strongly that each of my students could excel during this unit in mime, maybe not with every technique or activity, but before the unit was over, they could experience this silent art with success. I found the following techniques and activities a great way to demonstrate the use of one's entire body without the use of one's voice. I wanted my students to:

- Be introduced to a new way of communicating through the use of mime.
- Broaden their awareness of how we speak with our bodies in everyday life.
- Understand how their body language helps them interact and communicate ideas, emotions, and stories.
- Know there is a variety of ways of completing these activities.

A Short History

It is difficult to trace the history of mime because the "mimes" left very little written material about their work, as it was a performing art, not a literary one. The art of mime has come down to us through the centuries in very personal ways: father to son, master to apprentice, and clown to clown.

Mime is one of the earliest modes of communication. The first cave people acted out their daily experiences through pantomime. They believed in pantomiming their successful hunts, even exaggerating their abilities.

Greek historians trace mime back to 500 B.C. and credit the simplest definition to Aristotle's use of the word *mimesis,* which simply means *to imitate life*. The Latin word *pantomimus* came from the Greek words *panto,* (all) and *mimus* (to mimic or copy).

During the Roman Empire, mimes became solo performers using themes from mythical, epic, and tragic sources. In most cases, they used either solo or choral narration and/or music accompaniment. There was one famous Roman mime, Livius Andronicus, who was compelled to be silent during one of his performances because he had lost his voice temporarily. Due to the favorable reaction of his audience, he decided to adopt silence as his particular style.

After the fall of the Roman Empire, the art form was kept alive by wandering mimes throughout the Middle Ages. Its strongest reappearance occurred in the 1500s in Italy by way of the commedia dell'arte (artists of comedy). These performers could act, sing, do acrobatics, and play instruments. Their plays appealed to the common man. There was much chasing, running into walls, and falling. The Keystone Cops are a prime example of commedia.

The various commedia plays always centered on the fool, Arlecchino/Harlequin, an engaging clown who was always chasing a young woman, often referred to as Columbine. Commedia traveled all over Europe influencing styles of theatre wherever they traveled. A part of this traveling troupe became what we know of today as the circus.

The French had the strongest contribution to the art of mime through the efforts of Jean-Gaspard Deburau (1796-1846). Deburau was a young Bohemian who performed with his family of acrobats in Paris. In 1852, his son Charles combined many of the qualities of the commedia characters into one character named Pierrot. It is through this role that many people today accept him as the father of classical silent mime. Pulcinella, another character from commedia, became the forerunner of "Punch" in the "Punch and Judy" puppet shows of the English Pantomimes.

The two men who refined twentieth century mime were Etienne Decroux and Jean-Louis Barrault. They used their bodies exclusively to express life through "illusions." Without props, scenery, or sound, they were able to present the physical world. For example, they could move their bodies in such a fashion that the spectators were convinced they were walking, running, or being pushed by an imaginary wind with a limited amount of movement.

One of Decroux's students was Marcel Marceau, who became the world's most popular mime and exponent of the art of silent mime. Thanks to YouTube, all can view his mimes.

Group Warm-Ups

Stressing Emotions and the Environment

This group warm-up helps students become aware of how their bodies move in a particular situation. Have your class spread out in the classroom and move about the space, without talking or physical contact with each other. Then give them the walks described below, reminding them not to talk, just "do."

After doing several of the walks below, stop and ask, "Could you feel any physical difference between the walks? Which was the easiest?" You want them to realize that emotions and environment do affect how we move.

Walking on:
- The moon
- Jell-O
- A narrow log over a crocodile-infested river
- Deep snow
- Spaghetti
- The bottom of the ocean with weights on your feet

Walking as if they felt:
- Angry
- Athletic

- Confused
- Enthusiastic
- Frightened
- Jumpy

Now as they are walking, they are feeling or sensing various types of weather:
- Blinding snowstorm
- Bright sunshine
- Dark woods
- Downpour
- Hurricane winds
- Sweltering heat

Now they are walking on their way to:
- A police car after being arrested for shoplifting
- A wedding
- An audition
- The principal's office
- Their execution
- Their first job

Statue

Playing the child's game of Statue is a great way to get your students up and moving. It is nonthreatening and your students will start becoming aware of how their bodies move. It works best with a group of six to eight. Have them move about the room, swinging arms, jumping, bending, something very active, and call "Freeze." Then one by one have your students motivate their frozen pose and continue with whatever activity they think the pose represents. By the way the movement is executed we will know what they are doing. After each student completes his or her action, discuss what everyone saw. Sometimes suggestions can be given of how to improve, but most of the time your students' actions are very clear.

Picture Game

This also works well with groups of six to eight. The performing group stands outside a designated performance space. One person runs into the space, forms his or her body into a statue, and announces what he or she is. For example, "I'm a mannequin in the store window."

Instantly, the next person runs in and forms something else in the same picture not saying what they are until everyone in the group has completed the whole picture. It should be clear to the audience what or who each addition is to the picture. If there is any confusion, the actors can say what they are, such as "I'm a shopper" or "I'm a saleslady." As soon as the picture is complete, begin with a new group. The picture can also be non-human like a park, including a tree, bench, etc. This game needs to go very, very fast.

Basic Mime Techniques

Following are the basic techniques I used. Of course, today you will find DVDs of these techniques and many others as well as a variety of pantomime artists performing on YouTube.

After the above warm-ups are done, start working on the following techniques. I did not spend an entire period on these techniques. I introduced two techniques, talking for about ten minutes. Each day we reviewed what we had learned the day before and then we'd go on to new techniques. Then I would intersperse the techniques with the activities listed below.

```
Before beginning any of the techniques below,
be  sure  your  students  understand  the  term
neutral: it is standing with their knees bent,
their  feet  flat  on  the  ground,  shoulder  width
apart, with their arms and hands hanging loosely
at their side.

When working with any of these techniques, it
would be wise to have really thin tennis shoes
or  anything  that  doesn't  have  much  sole.
Stocking feet work well. Heavy boots or flip-
flops do not work!
```

Profile Walk

Begin in neutral, your side to the audience. Put your weight on your left foot. Extend your right foot forward a comfortable distance, with your foot flat on the ground, weight still on your left foot. Your right knee remains straight as you slide your right foot back to your left foot. As your right foot slides back, lift your left heel off the ground by bending your left knee. Roll your weight onto the ball of your right foot. The sliding of your right foot and lifting of your left heel happen simultaneously.

Shift your weight to your right foot. Extend your left foot forward, knee straight. Sliding your left foot back into place, bend your right knee and lift your right heel. Now shift your weight onto the ball of your left foot, releasing your right for another step. Repeat the movement until it is smooth. Slide and lift, then shift. Be sure to keep your head and torso level; feel the action in your pelvis and legs. Let your arms follow the movement naturally.

Sliding Walk

If you happen to be a skier, this walk is very similar to the movement you do with your feet when cross-country skiing. Begin in neutral, facing your audience. Bend your right knee forward, lifting your right heel. Your weight is on the ball of your right foot. Straighten your right knee, lowering your right heel. As your right heel touches the floor, slide your left foot behind you, as if wiping something off your shoe. Bring your left foot around and forward in a small arc, back to its starting place, landing on the ball of your left foot.

Your weight is now on your left foot. Straighten your left knee. As your left heel touches the floor, slide your right foot back, as you did with the left. Repeat, alternating legs, until the rhythm is smooth. Feel the movement in your hips and knees. Keep your head and torso level. Let your arms swing naturally, left arm forward as the right knee goes forward and right arm forward as the left knee goes forward.

Easy Walk

Stand in neutral with your feet about shoulder width apart, arms at your side, relaxed, with your side to the audience. Stand on tiptoes. Your weight is now on the balls of your feet. Think of your toes as glued to the floor. Only your heels will move in this walk. Both knees remain bent, not locked tight, and remember your toes are firmly glued in place. Raise your right heel, bending your right knee. Your knee will be going forward rather than upward. Feel the shift in your pelvis as your right hip moves forward too. The ball of your foot remains stationary; again, remember it is glued to the floor. As you lower your right heel, raise your left heel. Do this simultaneously. Don't wait for your right heel to settle before moving your left.

Repeat this, lowering your left heel, raising your right. All the action is taking place from your waist down. Your head remains level, not bobbing up and down. You want this movement to be smooth, not jerky.

Let your arms swing naturally with the movement. The left arm moves forward with the right knee and vice versa.

```
   For the following techniques, we will be using
the Easy Walk described above for the feet so
your  students  need  to  concentrate  on  their
hands, eyes, and back. They will also want to
visualize the object they are using, whether it
is a banister or rung.
```

Upstairs

Lean slightly forward, look up at the flight of stairs, and tightly grasp the banister at your right at shoulder height to maintain the shape. Slide your hand vertically down the banister and stop at your waist. You will stop when the heel of your right foot touches the floor.

Next, straighten your back and continue sliding your hand down the banister to hip level. Stop when your left heel touches the floor. Look up, bend your back, and reach for the banister, etc.

Downstairs

Look down at an imaginary banister at your left. Lean slightly backward, looking down the flight of stairs. Grasp the banister tightly at hip height to maintain the shape. Slide your hand vertically up the banister, stopping at your waist. You will stop when the heel of your left foot touches the floor.

Next, straighten your back and continue sliding your hand up the banister to chest level. Stop when your left heel touches the floor. Look down, lean back, and reach for the banister, etc. You can, of course, look back to see how far you have come!

Up a Ladder

You can do this one of two ways. Look up and grab the metal ladder by the sides with both your hands at shoulder height, your elbows resting on each side of your chest, about your hip's width apart. Slide your hands down nine inches. As you are sliding your arms down, take a step with your right foot. When your right heel touches the floor, you have moved your hands the nine inches. Then slide your hands down another nine inches, take another step, this time with your left foot. Your arms are stopped when your left heel touches the floor.

Then take your right hand off the ladder and put it back at shoulder level, then take the left hand and do the same. Take a step. And continue. If you take both hands off the sides, you will fall!

Some people prefer to use the rounded rungs of a wooden ladder. Starting with your right hand, look up and grab a rung, curling your hands around it at chin level. Then take your left hand and grab a rung nine inches directly above your right, curling your hand around that rung. Bring both curled hands straight down, maintaining the nine-inch space between the rungs. As your hands are moving down you are taking a step. Stop when the upper hand reaches chin level and your right heel has touched the floor. Your eyes follow your hands down.

Lift your right hand, now on the bottom rung. Remember, only one hand can be released at a time or you will fall! Look up and reach for the next rung. Curl your hands around the ladder rung. Your left hand is now at chin level, your right hand nine inches directly above it. Bring your hands straight down, maintaining the nine-inch space. You have also taken a step with your left foot. Your left heel will touch the floor when you stop. Continue. As you are getting higher up the ladder, you might want to look down to show how high you are climbing and how you feel about that: scared, proud, in a hurry, etc. You can add all these things as you get better at the skill.

Down a Ladder

For going down we will only use the metal ladder. Grasp the sides of the ladder with your hands at waist level, your right foot on tiptoes. Slide your hands up nine inches, pause when your right heel touches the floor.

Slide your hands up another nine inches, about shoulder height, with your left foot on tiptoes, pause when your left heel touches the floor. Lift your hands from the sides of the ladder, one at a time — you do want to fall! Place your hands again at waist level. Continue.

Up A Rope

This technique requires practicing both the arms and legs separately, then combining them.

Arms

Look up at the rope. Reach above your head, as far as is comfortable, almost at arm's length, with the right hand, palm open. Grasp the rope, closing your palm around the rope, leaving room for the rope. Now reach up with the left hand and grasp the rope, right under your right hand. Be sure your leave room in your grip for the rope! Slide both hands straight down toward your chest, keeping the size of the rope the same by tensing your hands around the imaginary rope before you move them. Stop. Hold your hands in position at chest level. Your knees get a new grip. Look up, then reach up with your right hand. Grasp the rope again. Follow with your left hand below it. Again, do not let both hands off the rope or you will fall. You are ready to pull down again.

Legs

Stand cross-legged holding the rope between your knees. Just before you begin to pull down, release the rope by opening or bending. You are lowering your knees down, sort of a squat; your knees are out to the side and standing on tiptoe. When your hands are at waist level, close your knees, grabbing the rope between your knees, and simultaneously lower your heels back to the floor. Lock your knees around the rope and hold. Let your hands get a new grip. You're ready to pull yourself up again.

Down A Rope

Practice arms and legs separately, then combine.

Arms

Grasp the rope at chest level, right hand above the left. Look down to where you're going. Slide both hands up until they are stretched above you, almost at arm's length. Release your hands one at a time and get a new grip on the rope back at chest level. You're ready to continue your descent.

Legs

Stand cross-legged, holding the rope tight between your knees. Just before you begin to pull up, release the rope by opening your knees out to the side and stand on tiptoe, or you will get a horrible rope burn! Grab the rope quickly between your knees and simultaneously lower your heels back to the floor. You're cross-legged again. Hold the rope there while your hands shift position and then release when your arms are pulling. You're ready to slide down again.

Evaluation

Now that your students have learned these basic techniques, they need to be graded. It was the first time I graded them on this unit. I again divided them into three or four groups and played a two-minute selection of circus music. Each group had to create a story, with a title, about a circus involving all the techniques: up and down a rope, up and down stairs, up and down a ladder, all the walks. They were to work together as well as alone. Each student in the group selected two techniques they would perform as a soloist; it could be going up and down a ladder or a walk and going up a rope, etc. The most challenging part of this assignment was to have all the techniques covered in the two-minute presentation.

Most of my students were very good at some of the techniques, but not every one of them. I felt it was unfair to grade students on something they physically could not get or could not do, even though they tried and tried. That is why I allowed them to be graded on the two techniques they felt they had mastered.

What was wonderful was how each group helped each other with the various techniques. There was always one person in each group who could do all the techniques. I always made sure of it! Watching each group not only solve who was the best at a specific technique, but also how they would tie everything into a story around a circus was one of the many joys of being a drama teacher.

Activities with Small Groups

Get into Groups

It can sometimes be hard to break the class into smaller groups without somebody being leftover, or the same people always working with each other, so why not make it into a game? An easy, nonthreatening activity is to call out a number and have your students get into groups of that number. If they don't have enough in their group, they should make it look like they are the right number of students by spreading themselves out, making the group look bigger. The number can be as big or small as you like. Towards the end, pick a number that is the size of the group you want for the next exercise.

The following smaller group activities continue using silent teamwork. They will be creating group pictures to tell a story. Have your students think about what makes an interesting group picture: body positions, gestures, facial expression, etc.

    Just as a reminder: for the following
    activities, divide your class into groups of
    four to six unless otherwise stated, making sure
    there are new groups each time there is a new
    activity.

Ten Second Objects

Select your groups and call out the name of an object. Each group has to make the shape of that object using their bodies, joining together in different ways while you count down slowly from ten to zero. Typically, every group will find a different way of forming the object. Examples could be a:
- Boat
- Car
- Clock
- Fire
- Fried breakfast
- Spaceship
- TV
- Washing machine

Frozen Pictures

Family Portraits

One group goes in front of the class and moves around for ten seconds. You then announce the family (ideas listed below) and immediately the group will create a frozen picture or portrait of that family. You can have each group do several portraits.

When you call "change," the first group leaves the acting area and the second group enters, moving around the room creating their family portrait. You could also have the following families on 3 x 5 cards and put in your card file. In that case, let the groups work separately and then freeze their picture and have the audience guess what family they are. Examples:
- A family of accountants
- A family of ballet dancers
- A family of bears
- A family of clowns
- A family of cooks
- A family of dogs or cats
- A family of fish
- A family of football, basketball, soccer, or tennis players
- A family of musicians
- A family of weightlifters

You could also have portraits of emotions. For examples:
- Frightened
- Happy
- Hungry
- Mad
- Sad
- Sick or ill

Photo Subjects

Have one group go up in front of the class and select one student to be a host. The rest of the group will be the photo subjects. The host chooses a subject (examples below) written on a 3 x 5 card and the group is given up to one minute — or more if you think they need it — to figure out what they will do. You might mention there can be several types of portraits: the one where everyone is perfect, the one where everyone is perfect except one, or the awkward family portrait. The host "clicks" to view the picture, the group freezes in their portrait, and the host then narrates what the portrait is about.

Examples:
• Birthday party
• Family reunion
• Funeral
• High school or college graduation
• Vacation (summer or winter)
• Wedding

Children's Stories

In advance, make up a list of children's stories — examples are listed below. Write each on a card and keep them in the 3 x 5 card file, so they can be used over and over.

Give each group a different card and allow them five minutes to decide on *three* frozen pictures that tell the whole story. You may need to coach, telling each group to be quiet. You do not want anyone else in the room to hear what they are doing. Every student is to participate in at least two of the three pictures. They can be people, chairs, trees, or anything the picture needs. As each group performs, the rest of the class has to figure out the story they are portraying.

Next, each group gets a new card and is given up to five minutes to create the story in *two* frozen pictures. Examples:
• Anything From Dr. Seuss
• *Beauty and the Beast*
• *Cinderella*
• *Emperor's New Clothes*
• *Goldilocks and the Three Bears*
• *The Tortoise and the Hare*
• *Little Red Riding Hood*
• *Pinocchio*
• *Sleeping Beauty*
• *Snow White*
• *Three Little Pigs*

Now, to add more difficulty, give each group another card, but this time you have selected nursery rhymes, which, of course, you have written on cards in advance. Everyone in the group is to be involved, but they can only do *one* frozen picture. Again, give them up to five minutes to create their pictures and then "perform."

Examples:
* *Hickory Dickory Dock*
* *Humpty Dumpty*
* *Jack and Jill*
* *Little Bo Peep*
* *Little Miss Muffet*
* *London Bridge Is Falling Down*
* *Ring-a-Round the Rosie*
* *There was an Old Woman Who Lived in a Shoe*
* *Three Blind Mice*

Silent Group Activity

After dividing your class into new groups, give them examples of an activity involving a group, such as a baseball game, a tour bus with guide, a shopping trip, eating pizza, or use a category, such as television shows, movies, sporting events, etc.

Each group will then go to a designated area of the room to discuss what they are going to do. They may not use any of the examples that were given and, of course, everything is silent. After five minutes, the groups will reassemble. Each group will perform their scene. After each performance, the audience speculates as to what was going on.

Fun Two- and Four-Person Activities

Mirrors

When you feel your class is ready to work in much smaller groups, introduce an exercise called mirrors, which helps students learn to take direction from their peers and a perfect way to teach concentration. Often after working on this for ten minutes, my students needed a break to shake out. We talked about why and they began to realize they were concentrating so hard they needed to stop.

Divide the class into pairs, sitting in their seats, facing each other. Start with the hands. One person is designated the leader and starts to *slowly* move his or her hands, palms up, and his or her partner follows along, palms of both students facing each other. They are never to literally touch each other, but their hands can be very close to each other. Allow this to go on for about thirty seconds and then say "switch."

Now the non-leader becomes the leader. Continue this exercise saying "switch" three or four more times.

As your students become more comfortable, encourage them to move their upper body, then have them stand up and move their whole body, incorporating facial expressions. You will continue to say "switch." Eventually the pairs are moving as one. Also have them change partners so they get a chance to work with several other students.

> Before you start this next series of mimes, you need to discuss appropriate behavior. Your students will be touching each other and they must do it *respectfully*. Safety can also be a concern; take time to discuss these issues with your class. You cannot stress this too much. Enough said.
>
> Start the following activities with the entire class and end with each student getting the opportunity to be a mannequin, robot, puppet, and clay.

Mannequin

Begin by having your class walk around your room with lots of energy, swinging arms, jumping, bending, etc. Call out "freeze." Your students should be so still, they give the illusion of a person who has been frozen in an action.

Now divide the class in half. Have one group up in front moving about with energy and say "freeze." This time when they freeze, have the students think about being a mannequin, a nonhuman, and try to make their frozen position look like a "dummy" in a store window display.

Have the next group come up and repeat the exercise. However, after you say "freeze," tell your students to not only look like mannequins, but to work with tension to hold the entire body still. The face cannot move. They might think of a doll's eyes trapped in a moment of time. Remind them again they are not human.

Next, have your class pair off. Discuss the mannequin's three joints:

- Neck that can only go from side to side, not up and down.
- Shoulder — not the elbow, wrist, or hand.
- Waist, which can only move from left to right, not bend forward or back.

Have one partner be a mannequin and the other the manipulator. The mannequin starts off in a pose. The manipulator stands behind or to the side of the mannequin and moves three joints. You do not want the manipulator to block the mannequin in any way. The manipulator can move both shoulders and the neck or just their neck, while the arms and waist are stationary. During this time, the mannequin's face and eyes cannot move. To help with focus, have the mannequin stare straight ahead at a spot on the wall.

Do not have your students work with the legs or knees. Ideally, you would pick the mannequin up and move it, but as this is not practical, be sure the mannequin has his or her legs planted solidly on the ground. Then, have the partners switch so everyone has a chance to be a mannequin and a manipulator.

Isolation Exercise

After your students have mastered the mannequin, begin with this simple exercise. Start by having your students mime chewing a wad of gum. After chewing it really well, have them take it out of their mouths and stick it to their knees. Have them grab the piece of the gum and lift their knee.

Now take the gum off the knee and stick it on their wrist. Again, they grab the piece of gum and lift their wrist. Continue this activity until all the major joints are "gummed." They have just done an isolation exercise, moving one part of the body at a time, the technique needed for doing a robot.

Robot

Have your class stand straight and rigid. Tell them they are now made out of solid units of metal, connected at a few main joints. Have them lift their right forearm in a series of three jerks. Snap into each movement, emphasizing the start and stop. Now have them lower their arms in the same way. It is a very jerky movement.

Next, test all their body parts, one by one. Keep in mind, only one part moves at a time, starting and stopping with precision. Using three jerks, have them move the following:
- Turning the head right, center, left.
- Bobbing the head up and down.
- Moving the shoulders up and down, not the neck or head.
- Moving the elbows and wrist up and down, not the shoulders.
- Turning the waist right, center, left.
- Bending forward, at the waist, keeping the back straight.
- Lifting the knee.

They have just created a machine, a nonhuman. Again, divide the class into groups of two. One will be a robot and the other the manipulator. Let the human press the robot's buttons, which are on an imaginary pad, so the audience can see what is happening. After working for several minutes, perform a little scene and then switch so each student gets to be a robot.

Marionette/Puppet

We will continue working with isolation, but instead of being made of metal, we are now made of spaghetti or string. Your students are to imagine they have air between all their joints. Have the class stand up and then bend over at the waist. Their knees are bent slightly — spaghetti doesn't have much body! Their heads hang down, arms dangling loosely. The body is relaxed.

Now have them picture an invisible puppeteer or manipulator tugging the string at the center of their backs. Remind your students they are no longer robots. Instead of jerky movement, all movements will be bouncing or wobbling up and down. The manipulator pulls their back string so they are now standing upright, not stiff, but very wobbly, knees bent. Let your students try the following, reminding them an invisible manipulator is doing the pulling, and the face and eyes do not move:

- Your head string is slowly pulled up until your face is forward and chin parallel to the floor. Your head settles in with a wobble.
- Your head falls forward; the string is dropped!
- Your head string is pulled in a circle, and then around again to the other side.
- One shoulder string pulls your shoulder up and forward and then back while your arm remains limp. Rotate the other shoulder.
- Both shoulders are raised together and then they are pulled in opposite directions. One string pulls an elbow up to shoulder height. Your wrist and forearm dangle loosely.
- The wrist string lifts your forearm up and spins it like a windmill. The string lets loose and your arm falls down. Repeat with other arm.
- Your wrist strings lift both arms out to the sides and up to shoulder height. Your hands rotate forward, pulled by the strings on the back of them. They are going faster, then your arm strings are let go and they fall at your side.
- One knee string pulls up and rotates your upper leg.
- Your ankle string tugs forward to rotate your calf and foot. Then the string in the center of your foot lifts and rotates it. Slowly, your imaginary puppeteer loosens your knee string until you are standing again on two feet.

- All strings on the right side pull up. The other side slumps down. Now the left side strings are lifted.
- All the strings holding the top of your body are cut loose. Slump. You are as you began, a lifeless marionette.

Again, have your class pair off, one the puppet and one the manipulator, and try to do some simple movements. The manipulator stands on a chair behind the puppet and pulls his or her strings. The puppet is actually the one initiating the movement, and the puppeteer follows. It is usually best if the two confer as to what is going to happen first. The puppet must move slowly, so the manipulator can create the illusion of strings being pulled. The real trick is to keep the strings the same length as you move the joints up and down. Then, of course, change places.

Clay

Now, with new pairs, begin a sculpting exercise. One of the students is a piece of clay and the other is the sculptor. The student playing the piece of clay is to remain very still and relaxed, but to conform to the way their body is positioned by the sculptor. They can lie on the ground, sit in a chair, or stand. After they are molded, they are to hold that position.

Again, emphasize how important it is to treat the clay gently and with respect. Your sculptors must be very careful and considerate at all times when molding their clay. Remember, the clay has to hold that position for some time.

Your students may want to create a statue, shape, or action with their clay. As they are sculpting, they need to keep the audience's point of view in mind. They want their audience to believe that they are indeed working with a lump of clay and are making something out of it. Therefore, the sculptor needs to hide the "lump" when "molding" by standing directly in front of it, showing the audience their back muscles as they create their work of art. When their creation is finished, they stand away and the audience sees the final product. Then reverse. The sculptor becomes clay and the clay becomes the sculptor.

Evaluation

An ideal way to end this small mime unit and evaluate it is to have your class divide into groups of four, creating a mime, using all the above techniques. It should have a title and be at least two minutes in length. Everyone must be at least one thing. One person cannot be a manipulator all the time. Base your grading on enthusiasm, technique, believability, and total performance. Music can enhance the effect.

> Be aware when you give students time to discuss what they are going to do with a specific activity. They tend to spend too much time talking about what they are going to do and not enough time *doing it*. Get them up and active.
>
> When teaching up at the MCT Summer Camp, my students, with only thirty minutes of practice, developed a two-minute presentation to music. You can see one of the groups on my website: margaretfjohnson.com. Click on "Photos" and scroll to the section "Robots, Mannequins, and Puppets."

Solo Activities

Four Imaginary Objects

Select any four imaginary objects such as a cat, a window, a door, and a puddle. The goal for each of your students is to create a scene using all these objects. The first student goes up in front of the class and performs his or her mime. After he or she has finished, ask the audience, "What happened? Was the story clear?" Next, another student creates a different scene using the same imaginary objects. Continue, as above, remembering your students may not repeat earlier performances. All those in the audience will have a turn, hopefully! You may need to change the objects if you have a large class.

Masks

I had the opportunity to see Marcel Marceau live — one of the most exciting evenings of theatre I have ever attended. One of his mimes dealt with his character trying on various masks. In the end, the last mask is stuck and he could no longer take it off.

This got me to thinking about having my students do an exercise where they had to put on and take off four different masks. The trick was to show us:

- Getting the mask off an imaginary wall.
- Holding the mask in their hands.
- Putting it on, showing the entire class the mask.
- Taking the mask off.
- Replacing it back on the wall.

That was the first part of the assignment. One problem my students had was keeping their faces neutral or in one specific expression. The second part of the assignment was to show all four masks without putting them on.

The students needed to cover their faces with their hands. When they opened their hands, their first mask was revealed. Then the hands cover the face again, and when the hands were removed, the second mask was revealed, and so on until all four masks were exposed. Now, that wasn't too difficult, was it? Well … the point was to show us all four masks four times in order, as fast as possible!

Have your students give their masks names or expressions such as happy, sad, dumb, wide awake, etc., which helps change them rapidly. Some of my students were absolutely wonderful and could do it very quickly, but the majority did well. This is a great concentration activity.

Solo Evaluation

For the Four Imaginary Objects exercise, I gave a blanket grade.
I divided the grading for the Masks into two parts:
• Putting on the masks.
• Switching the masks.

I never failed students who tried — maybe they were very unsuccessful, but they had given it their all. On the other hand, if you just want to give them a grade for attempting the exercise, that's fine too. As it was early in the quarter, asking your students to do something this difficult by themselves was too much. I usually gave the same grade to anyone who truly attempted the assignment. If students were exceptional, I would give them several extra points.

Unit 5
Stage Fighting

Fights have played a crucial role in theatre tradition ever since the days of Roman tragedies. We also know William Shakespeare included stage combat as one of the many innovations in his plays. Stage fighting had a resurgence with the advent of the silent movies and today has taken on a life of its own. And students love doing it!

There are many fighting techniques. I found these worked best in my classroom: throwing slaps or punches, pulling hair, choking, kicking, and performing *The Three Stooges'* eye poke — a standard for slapstick comedy. Check out YouTube, it has great clips.

Before you begin this great unit, there are four very important things to remember:

- The first, and most important, thing about stage fighting is safety. You don't ever, ever, ever hit or make contact with anybody. You're always hitting around or faking it in some way to trick the audience. That's why it's *stage* fighting.
- As I mentioned earlier, before you begin this activity, you need to discuss *appropriate behavior.* Your students will be touching each other and they must do it *respectfully.*
- Thirdly, have your pairs plan what they will be doing so they both know what is to happen. Always have an outline or a very good idea of the specific action. If they do not plan it out, their fight is going to be very unsafe, and someone is going to get hurt. Never make up a fight on the spot.
- Before your students start "fighting," you need to have a clear space so if they fall, slip, or trip, they're not going to knock books off a shelf, hit their heads on a desk, etc.

Preparing for Stage Fighting

After the basics above have been covered, go over the following guidelines with your students before they do any kind of slapping or punching:

"You must establish a distance between you and your partner. Begin by going up and putting your hands on your partner's shoulders to establish a safe distance, so you're not too close or too far away. You want the slap or punch to look real.

You must make eye contact. This is very important because it is the cue between you and your partner, letting him or her know you are about to carry out the attack you have planned in advance."

After your students have established a safe distance and maintained eye contact, you're almost ready to teach them how to do a punch and slap. But wait ... there are three more things you need to say to your students:

"Before you hit anyone, you want to form an imaginary frame around his or her face. You want to slap or punch outside of the frame.

You never want to just slap and stop. You always want a good follow through, so the audience believes you actually threw a punch or slap.

You must work slower than you actually would if you were really hitting somebody. You want your fight to go slowly, so you can get the physical movement down and memorize it. Your audience is there to watch the action, not watch someone get hurt. Overexaggerate your movements. When you are ready, you will not go at 100%, but rather 75% of the actual speed. You always want to be in control."

Now, *finally,* we can get to the actual fight!

```
    For the purpose of simplification, you, the
reader, will always be the aggressor and your
victim will be poor Sally Glutz. She isn't a
nice person!
```

Slapping and Punching

Sally has just accused you of something horrible. She needs to be slapped! Put your left hand on Sally's right shoulder, make eye contact with her, and swing your right arm back with your palm open, then continue the arc in front of her face, in the frame you have created. As soon as you start your swing with the right arm, drop your left arm, because when you follow through, you're going to be hitting your right hand with the palm of your left hand. That is what makes the hitting sound. Sally puts her left hand up to her left cheek and reacts to the hit.

The only difference between a punch and a slap is your hand. A slap has an open hand and a punch has a fisted hand. So again, hand on the shoulder, eye contact, rear back with a punch, and follow through.

Another way of making the sound is to have Sally slap her own hands as your hand "hits her face." This can be a problem, because often the clapping comes after the fake hit and the illusion of the slap is missed.

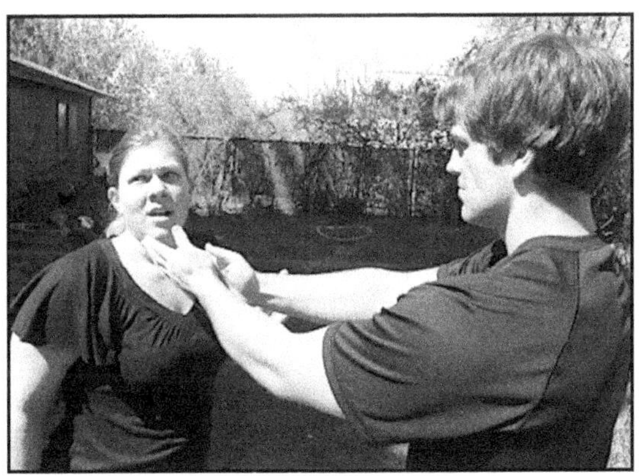

Hair Pulling

If you are really ticked off at Sally, you might want to pull her hair. A very important thing about the hair pull is that you, the attacker, are never in control. The attackee, Sally, is. Establish your distance, just like you did for the slap, making sure you have eye contact before you start. Now lift your right arm, with a very nasty look on your face, and go over the top of Sally's head with your hand splayed open.

As you come down on her head, make contact with her hair with the palm of your hand. At the same time, take your fingers and ball them into a fist with your fingers curled into your palm. Lay your balled-up hand on top of her head. Sally then takes over. Her hands go up on your wrist or forearm, and as you push away from her head, she pushes your hand into her head. She is in total control. She looks like she's in pain. She decides when it's over — she will let go. You did not move a muscle — she did the whole thing. This is very important to remember, because if you start using some control, you could hurt her. Always remember to go slow at first and then you can speed up.

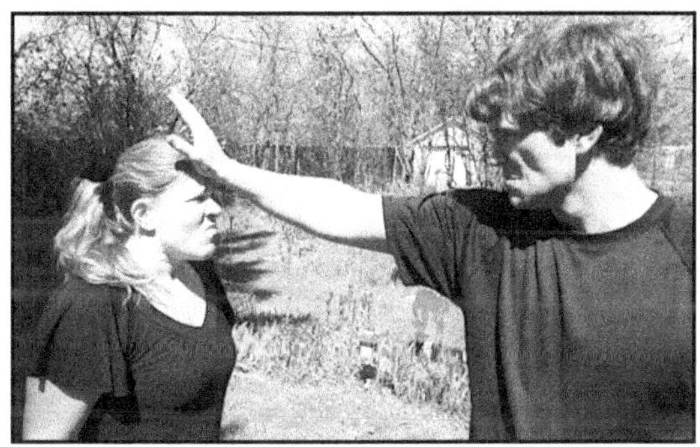

Choking

Sally won't be quiet. You want her to be quiet, so you decide to choke her. The first thing you want to do, I repeat, is have eye contact between you and Sally. You will move in with both arms and your fingers splayed, but this time you are going to wrap them around her throat. You can come in from the side or the front, whichever works best for you.

When you have your hands around her throat, she's going to grab your wrist or forearms and again, just like the hair pull, she's in control. As you press in to her throat to choke her, she pulls your hands away from her throat. She is essentially choking herself. Her hands are protecting her neck. Of course, there is acting going on. Sally is losing air, she tries to get away. She decides when to stop and lets go when she is done.

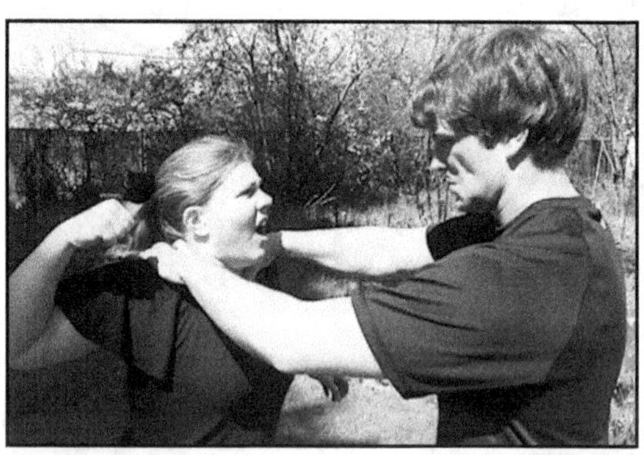

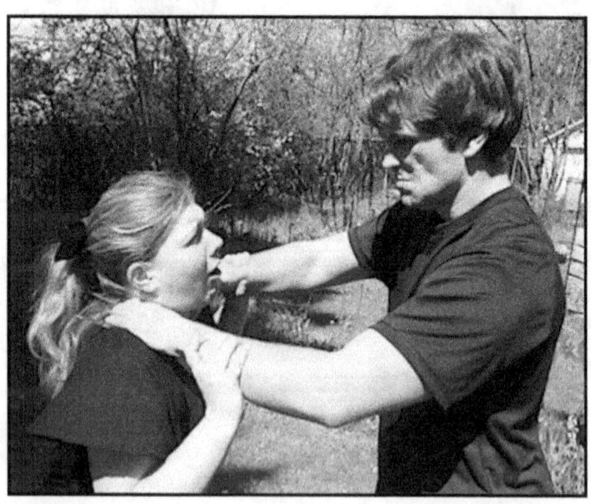

Kicking Someone When They Are Down

For some reason you're a real jerk and want to kick Sally while she's down. You notice she is on the ground, her back to the audience. Instead of actually kicking her, which you never do, *you never ever hit anyone*, you're going to kick the ground instead. Pick up your foot, rearing back, letting the audience know you're going to kick her, and then kick the ground directly in front of Sally. Her body blocks the fake kick.

She immediately reacts accordingly, going into the fetal position and making horrible noises. From the audience's point of view, it looks like you just kicked her in the stomach, while she was down, and you're a horrible person.

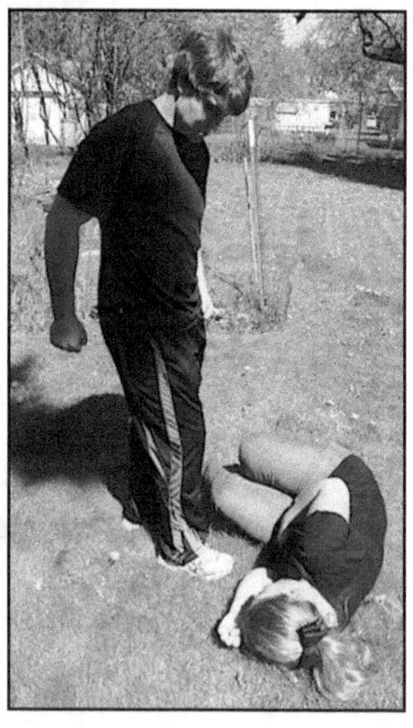

Eye Poking

Nothing has worked! Sally is still being a problem, so you resort to the eye poke. Again, establish distance and eye contact. You'll be using two fingers on your right hand. Your left arm remains on Sally's shoulder, getting your distance just right. Wind up with the right arm, go way back, and come over the top of Sally's head, landing right on her forehead, far away from her eyes.

Press or push off. Sally immediately puts her hands over her eyes and reacts. Sally's back is facing the audience, blocking the action. However, if you get very good at this, it can be done to the side. Remember, the audience doesn't know what is going to happen and if it is fast enough, they can be fooled.

Evaluation

The following two assignments work well to evaluate your students' stage fighting techniques.

Improv Scene with Sound

Allow your students to work in pairs on an improv using at least two of the techniques you have just taught them. Besides reminding them about planning out their fight, make it very clear this is a school setting, so various types of language are not appropriate. Also caution them to be sure they are aware of where the audience is and to be sure to block the fake hits. We, the audience, want to believe that someone is being hurt, when in reality it is all fake. Often two groups can work together, helping each pair make sure the audience does not see all fake hits, eye pokes, etc.

Mini Silent Movie

Begin this assignment by showing a short Charlie Chaplin film found on YouTube. Discuss the overacting, the slapstick, and exaggeration of face and body. Next, play a piece of silent movie music, approximately two minutes long. You can find some great pieces free of charge on the Internet.

Divide your class into groups of three to five. Each group is to create a mini silent movie, which can be performed with the music. The scene must have a policeman, a thief, and a shop owner, incorporating at least two of the fake fighting techniques described above. Remind them not to forget their movie should have a strong beginning, middle, and end as well as strong characters.

Each group is also given two pieces of card stock to create placards and a large black marker, which must be used appropriately! Play the music several times, then allow about fifteen minutes for each group to plan their movie. We don't want anyone to be hurt. Replay the music allowing each group to coordinate the music with their story.

As these two assignments will each take a day, if you do both of them, be aware of time. You want each group to be able to perform before the bell rings. If you have an exceptional pair of fighters or a great silent movie, you might consider having them perform in the cafeteria or the hall at the end of day. Of course, this must be cleared though the administration.

Unit 6
Several Solo and Duo Acting Activities

If it still is too early for solo work, several of the activities listed below can work as duos. When two people want to do these together, you could allow double the time for the performance.

Personal Commercial

As one of your first solo graded assignments, have the students create a thirty-second commercial about him or herself. It can take any form: a testimonial, a song and dance, a slice of life, multiple characters, etc. It can be anything as long as it is in commercial form and does not exceed thirty seconds. If two people want to do this together, you could allow up to one minute for the performance.

Name Cheer

This is a great homework assignment. The students are to create a cheer using their first name. They are to do one motion or action with each letter of their name. A less stressful version is to have them do only one motion or action with their name. You could also add an alliterative adjective with the movement or action such as Sorrowful Sue or Chatty Cathy. This works well with two people.

Academy Award Game

Students come forward one at a time to give a brief acceptance speech. Students must:
- Say at least two sentences.
- Thank at least three people.
- Mention the title of the film or play for which they received the award.

It should only take about thirty seconds per student.

Commercial

An excellent duo activity is to create a new product to be released on the market shelves in the near future. It can also be a solo assignment. Give your students three to five minutes to present the product, explain it, and attempt to sell it. They must use their imaginations, but remember it is on sale in the high school — not everything may be appropriate!

Deciding on the Product

Your students need to consider the following three points:

• There must be a need for the product.

• The audience should benefit from purchasing their product.

• The audience must be able to afford their product.

After they have decided what their product is going to be and you have cleared it, they need to think about the following:

• *Belief in their product.* To sell a product to an audience you must be sold on the product itself. If you think it's great, it is easier to convince your listeners.

• *Need for their product.* Tell your audience why they need this item. How will buying your product help them? What can the product do for them? Why will life be better for them if they purchase it? For example, will the water jet cut down on their tooth cavities? Can they get the fruitcake to Granny before Christmas? Will the safety features of your product really protect them?

• *Know their product.* How does it work? What is it made of? Know the available colors and the cost. Does it have any special features? Is it better than similar products already on the market? Is there a guarantee? Can it be repaired?

• *Demonstrate their product.* Show how it works. Show the results. Pass around a sample, if possible.

• *Make it easy to buy.* State the price of your product. Tell where it can be purchased. Is there a down payment? Can the buyer get a discount on a trade-in? Is there a rebate? Is this a limited special and/or will the buyer receive a free gift with purchase? Can they buy it right now? Can they give you an order?

• *Close the commercial with a catchy ending.* Do or say something relevant to the product that the audience will remember. For example, a surprise ending to the commercial or a singing jingle.

Music can set the mood. Your students may wish
to use background music or a song to set the
mood for the commercial.

Writing the Script

The next thing your students need to do is write their script
following the simple steps listed below. Again, they need to use
their imaginations!

- First, write a plot outline. This will tell what is to happen in the commercial and in what order.
- Is this commercial humorous or serious? This will determine the characters and the dialogue.
- Decide on who will sell the product. Will it be one person or two? Give the character(s) name(s), if possible. What are these people like? What will the actor have to know about the character in order to play him or her accurately?
- Decide whether the setting is important. If it is, describe it. What will need to be made or brought from home to create the setting?
- Start writing at the beginning, not in the middle or the end!
- Begin writing the dialogue (two people) or monologue (one person). Try to make the words fit the character. For example, an actor who is wearing dirty overalls, a straw hat, and chewing on a straw would probably not say, "I'm here to render my opinion as to the effects of gamma rays on the protein nucleus of the particulate ZX1." Likewise, a man in a pinstriped suit, with a briefcase in his hand would probably not look up from the *Wall Street Journal* and say, "Hey, that's rad! What's happenin'? Put er there, brother!"
- Be sure to review those points you considered earlier.
- Write out all of the stage directions completely. Where is/are the actor(s) supposed to move? When? How do you demonstrate the product?
- Remember to use your creative abilities! Be as funny or as serious as you wish; just sell us your product.

After their scripts are written, you need to review them. Then decide on the presentation order, maybe use the numbers and hat methods mentioned on page 96.

Evaluation

For the three short solo activities mentioned above, each could be worth more than the succeeding one, showing growth and expertise.

For the commercial, you have to decide what you think this assignment is worth. Is it as important as the mask assignment or a solo monologue? There is a writing component to this assignment. I always divided the grading into two parts: the actual performance and the script. I felt both were equally important.

Another element to the grading might involve your audience. Did they really want to buy this product? Maybe create a simple rubric using numbers from one to ten that the audience has to fill out after each presentation is given, adding up the points to see how successful each product was.

Unit 7
Working with Monologues

A Ten Day Assignment Using
Monologues for Character Development

It is now time for the physical movement and the vocal exercises you explored earlier to come together to create a character using monologues. This character may be speaking his or her thoughts aloud, directly addressing another character, or speaking to the audience. Not only should your students be concerned with their vocal approach, but they also need to consider how the character stands, sits, and moves. In my semester class, I began this late in the first quarter when everyone had experienced choral reading and mime and was comfortable getting up in front of the class.

You will need a collection of monologues, a class set of a monologue book, or a play with many solo parts. Today there are excellent monologue books available for middle school as well as high school. Meriwether Publishing has many from which to choose.

You will want your students to do their pieces more than once. It is very important, whenever possible, that your students get a chance to truly explore their characters. By doing the piece several times, they can see their characters in different ways. They also will become much more at ease with their memorization and the final presentation will be something they can be very proud of. Even today, years after having had my drama class, students can still recite their *Spoon River* piece.

As we all know, acting is so much more than just memorization. I think we do our students a disservice by having them present a monologue or a scene only once or twice.

The way I approached this assignment was to use Charles Aidman's adaptation of Edgar Lee Masters' *Spoon River Anthology.* However, these activities can be modified to any set of monologues. Remember, a play is about people. My major concern with young actors was to work with character.

Day 1: Reading the Script

Begin by discussing the characters of *Spoon River* in general. These people represented a whole town in the middle of the 1800s, including crooked politicians, ladies of the evening, and drunks. Playing these disgraceful characters is such fun, because in real life, your students aren't these people. Caution them that if they know their parents will object to them playing disreputable characters, they have over fifty characters to pick from. One parent called and informed me his daughter was not going to play a whore! Pass out your class set of *Spoon River* and have the students read the script, writing down three characters they would like to portray. At the end of the period, collect the scripts so they will be available the next day and after school.

Day 2: Selecting the Monologue

The students continue reading for about twenty minutes, and then the selection process begins. You have prepared a sheet of paper ahead of time that includes a list of all the characters and the pages on which their solos appeared. Those with ten lines or fewer you have marked in bold. Most of the characters in *Spoon River* had between sixteen and twenty lines. You want all the students to be on a level playing ground. If a student chose a character from the bolded list, they knew they would be graded differently.

Next, select the characters by reading down the list of characters you have prepared earlier. If only one student raises his or her hand when a character's name is read, he or she gets his or her character. If two or more students want a specific character, select a number between one and twenty and the one who comes closest gets the character. This is the fairest way of deciding. Continue down the list until every student has chosen a character. Often after going through the whole list some students change their minds.

```
    I did not want two students doing the same
monologue. It is always interesting to see how
two different people look at a specific
character, but I did not want my students
comparing performances: "his was so much better
than mine," or "I'm soooo much better than
Sally."
```

After the solos are selected, have your students take out a clean sheet of paper, put the name of the character and the page he or she appeared on at the top, and carefully copy the monologue. From this copy, they are going to read, memorize, and write an analysis of their character. It has to be correct. If they do not have enough time, try to be available during lunch and after school for students to come in and finish writing. You need to keep the scripts in your class because you have more than one class using them.

Day 3: Making Memories

Included in the Appendix on page 159 is my form Making Memories/How to Learn and Recall. Discuss the importance of memorization: getting all the lines correct, not paraphrasing the author's words. Memorizing is just the first step in the acting process and only after their piece is memorized can real acting begin. You might discuss what works for you. Word association is the good one to use after the basic idea of the line is understood.

Make sure everyone is caught up. If some need still more time to copy the piece, allow them to do so and those who have their piece copied can start the memorization process.

When I was playing Peter Quince in *A Midsummer Night's Dream*, I could not remember the order of the three requests: "But masters, here are your parts: and I am to entreat you, request you and desire you to … " I made the acronym *of the three words*. When I got to that part of the line, I just thought of *erd* and the three words came to mind.

When playing Martha in *Arsenic and Old Lace*, I *could not* remember the line, "We weren't planning to go until … " but I could remember the word *scan*, rhyming with plan. Each night of performance, when Jonathan gave me my cue, I always remembered *scan* and the line came immediately.

Next, they read through the piece and make sure they understand what all the words mean. You are there for help, along with several dictionaries. The students then turn their paper over if there was not room at the bottom and write a concise paraphrase of their piece. Of course, a discussion of paraphrasing is done. As this was poetry, sometimes it proved to be a very difficult assignment. For the rest of the hour, they write their paraphrase, ask for help if needed, and either start or continue working on their memorization.

Before grading any of your students' efforts, do the following Helpful Exercises as well as review your rules for participation.

Helpful Exercises

As soon as class starts and roll is taken, have the students take out their pieces and practice them quietly. Then, have them move to various corners of the room and speak their piece out loud while talking to the wall, floor etc.

Next, call out various emotions and characters and have them say their piece as being:

- Children
- Cheerleaders
- Happy
- Mad
- Old people, who are deaf
- Sad
- Scared
- Sexy
- Stupid

Yes, the room is very, very noisy, but no one is put on the spot and they are rehearsing. When they are working specifically on memorization, add working with a partner for about five minutes.

Rules for Participation

10 Second Rule

I never called on my students. They were to volunteer. I gave them ten seconds to get up. Any more time and I felt class time was wasted. They had to make up their own minds about doing or not doing the assignment. If no one got up, then whoever had not gotten up would receive a zero. Yes, to answer your question, there were classes and students who tested me. And yes, they received a zero, but interestingly, the next day they did perform!

Pick a Number

If the ten second rule seems too extreme, another option is assigning each student a number. Maybe it is the number in the grade book or a random number from one to thirty. You write the corresponding number next to their name and use that number throughout the year. For each new assignment, fill a cup or hat with these numbers.

Volunteers

There will almost always be one or two students who will volunteer right away. After they perform, and no one else volunteers, the student who presented last picks a number from the cup or hat. The student whose name is selected can choose to go up and perform or take a zero and another number is drawn, and so on. The students always do the number selecting.

Draw a Number

At the beginning, if no one volunteers, have a student draw a number and that person will get up and perform if he or she chooses to do so. When he or she is done, he or she picks the next number, and so on.

Learning to Critique Fellow Students

Several things I know you're wondering about are: "What do I do with those students who are just watching the activity? I need to make this an educational experience for them too. I want them to pay attention, becoming a part of the whole process of theatre by being a good, informed audience."

We need to teach our students to view acting with a critical eye when watching fellow actors. The downfall is that sometimes our students become overly critical or very generous. Criticism is so helpful and much needed in the arts, but learning how to do it and accept it takes practice.

Praise Sandwich

One way to start the process of criticism is by a constructive feedback technique called a praise sandwich. The bread is the praise and the filling is the criticism. Always start and end with the "good stuff" just as you do when you make a sandwich.

Student Evaluation Form

Another way to criticize is to use a form your students in the audience fill out. I have included a sample Student Evaluation Form in the Appendix on page 161. This is a great way to start your students in becoming good evaluators. Yes, they had to be respectful of each other, but they also needed to become good adjudicators.

Sometimes I would only have a select group evaluate each performer, but I made sure everyone, each day, had to adjudicate at least one class member.

```
I am giving the assignment on the day it was
performed. You, of course, will assign it the
day before. You could also print out a calendar
of the unit's dates and performances and hand it
out the first day of the unit.
```

Day 4: Reading Their Piece

Start with the helpful exercises mentioned above. The students present their characters for the first time by reading their piece. They need to work vocally and have practiced it enough so they do not stumble and have all the words pronounced correctly. Peoria was a difficult word to pronounce. I never hesitated to correct them, but tried to do it after they had finished their reading. A discussion then ensues over paraphrase. Take one of the pieces the students are not presenting and as a class create the paraphrase.

Day 5: Paraphrasing and Character Analysis

The students read their paraphrase. If there were any questions, they explain their piece to the class, often referring back to the original piece. You could combine the reading and the paraphrase. Then you could spend Day 5 on the analysis and some memorization.

Pass out the Character Analysis for "Spoon River Anthology" sheet provided in the Appendix on page 162. This may take a great deal of time to explain. The students immediately realize numerous questions on the form are not specifically given in their piece and many questions arise. It's best to help them fill out the first two questions as a class by going around the room giving a bit of individualized instruction. You also need to state that there are no wrong answers — provided they have truly understood their piece. The analysis is due on Day 8.

Day 6: First Memorization

After doing your helpful exercises, explained above, it is time to perform. Explain prompting, providing actors with their lines, before you start. Each performer can give their piece to another student for prompting. Explain they are allowed two prompts per performance without having their grade reduced.

Give the students as much time as they need to begin their piece, but once they start, they have to continue. Stress that there are no do-overs. Explain, "In basketball, if a player tries to make a basket and doesn't make it, he or she cannot go up the referee and ask to do it over."

Day 7: Memorization with a Task

Now comes the time to do the monologue with a variety of activities. The first is a "doing" activity — we are expressing ourselves with movement. Explain that the task would not generally fit their character, but their job is to make the task the primary goal and the lines secondary. Obviously, not everyone can juggle or knit, for example, but tell him or her to do the very best he or she can. Students will be graded on how well they attempt the activity rather than having perfect memorization or skill with the activity.

Go around the room and quietly assign each student a task — some are listed below. Tell them they can bring any props that would help them complete the task. Once again, they can give their piece to another student for prompting; however, emphasize concentrating on the activity if they were having trouble with their lines. Generally, the lines will come. Of course, sometimes they don't!

Sample activities:
- Chewing gum
- Crying
- Drawing a picture
- Drinking five double lattes
- Drinking, of course non-alcoholic (I had a foreign exchange student come in to class with a can of beer. Yes, really!)
- Dusting

- Dying
- Eating
- Five different walks
- Itching
- Juggling
- Jumping
- Keeping cool
- Keeping warm
- Knitting
- Laughing
- Looking for a missing $100
- Making paper airplanes
- Opening a stuck wallet or purse
- Playing with a ball
- Pounding nails
- Putting on makeup
- Rearranging a room
- Ripping up a test paper
- Sleeping
- Smelling something and taking care of it
- Staying away from an ax murderer
- Stealing something
- Teaching a dance
- Touching everything in the room
- Trying to swat a fly or mosquito
- Using at least eight hand gestures
- Whining

Day 8: Memorization with a Specific Person

The next activity is a "being" activity — this time they should concentrate on their vocal abilities. You will be giving them a specific person to act like. Explain that this person would not generally fit their character, but the students' job is to make being the person the primary goal and the lines secondary. Obviously, not everyone can sing or dance, but again tell them to do the very best they can. They will be graded on how well they portray the person saying the lines from *Spoon River.*

    I also had another call from a parent not
    wanting her child to have anything satanic, like
    a vampire or ghost, so be sensitive to family
    values.

Go around the room and quietly assign each student a specific person or type of person. See the list below. You do not want the others in the class to overhear you, as the audience should be able to guess correctly whom they are when the performance is done. Tell them they can bring any props and/or costumes that would help them. Collect their analysis sheets and give them ten minutes to get ready.

Types of people:
- A four-year-old
- A ninety-year-old
- A person with an IQ of seventy-five
- A person with an IQ of one hundred eighty-five
- Airhead
- An insane person
- Any storybook character
- Bag lady
- Ballerina
- Beauty queen
- Coach
- Dracula
- Drill sergeant
- Farmer
- Gangster
- Ghost
- Guru
- Hard rock star
- Hippie
- Indiana Jones
- Lawyer
- Mad scientist
- Nerd
- Ninja turtle

- Opera star
- Person from outer space
- Personal trainer
- Pirate
- Professional wrestler
- Rapper
- Robin Hood
- Sheriff
- Superman
- Viking
- Western singer

Day 9: Memorization with Two Different Tasks

This again is a "being" activity. The students divide their piece in half, picking two of the following based on their Character Analysis of "Spoon River Anthology" (Appendix page 162): color, food, inanimate object, car, shoes, and/or animal. Students present their piece as what they think their chosen objects or animal would sound and move like. They can tell the audience what two things they were portraying, such as a color or food, but not the specifics.

After each performance is done, ask the audience what the student performed. Most of the time they will get it right. The performer then needs to justify why he or she chose their specific items. This is a difficult assignment but so worthwhile. The students have to really think about their characters and what they represent.

Now discuss why they had done the last three assignments. The students had been forced to use their voices and their bodies — what acting requires — and they now begin to see all the possibilities for developing a character. Pass back their Character Analysis of "Spoon River Anthology" sheet.

Day 10: Final Presentation

Today is the final presentation. They are "to be" their characters, both physically and vocally. They can bring in props and/or costumes if they choose. Give them ten minutes to prepare, change clothes, go over the piece, etc.

They are to start their character from the time they get up out of their seats until they sit back down, so how the character walks becomes important as well. The change from their first performance until their last is amazing.

Evaluation

Start with ten points for the reading and add five points each time they perform. Please, never fail any student who tries every activity, even if his or her performances are weak. I did the same evaluation for the second monologue as well.

A Seven-Day Assignment Using Modern Monologues

Doing one monologue was not enough exposure to solo acting. After *Spoon River,* the students needed to work on something modern. I purchased a class set of modern monologues with an even number of selections for boys and girls. Meriwether Publishing has a great selection.

Three points of caution, however:

- Be sure to read every piece in the collection. Do not give your parents room to complain. I have found some monologue books even my liberal community would have found troublesome.
- You have to be able to justify any piece in whatever book you choose.
- You do not want the pieces to be too serious — remember, students love angst!

Since I have already covered *Spoon River* in detail, the following are condensed descriptions for each day.

Day 1: Reading the Script

Students read the monologue book. As these are modern-day situations, not much time is spent on a discussion of the pieces.

Day 2: Monologue Analysis

Everyone makes their selections and writes their paraphrase. They start the memorization process and begin working in their Monologue Analysis on page 164 of the Appendix.

Day 3: Reading and Paraphrasing

Students read their piece to the class as well as their paraphrase. The rest of class time is spent working on memorization.

Day 4: Memorized

Today the students present their pieces memorized. Remember the Helpful Exercises provided earlier. Go around the room, assigning a person and a task, combining the two for a one-day assignment. Make sure your students do not get the same activities or person.

Day 5: Memorization with a Task and Person

Everyone presents his or her piece with a task and person. Again, do not forget the Helpful Exercises.

Day 6: Being a Color, Object, or Animal

Students present their piece as one of the three things they answered in their analysis — color, object, or animal — and turn in their Monologue Analysis sheet.

Day 7: Final Presentation

Today is the final presentation with costumes and props. The analysis is passed back.

A Four-Day Assignment Having Students Create Their Own Character

After working with two published monologues, or more if you want, it is now time to have your students create and write a monologue based on the answers given in the Analysis for Building Your Own Character on page 166 of the Appendix. We all had great fun with this activity. My students always begged me to do this again.

Day 1: Fill Out Analysis for Building Your Own Character

Begin by asking the students to take out a clean sheet of paper and be ready to write down some answers to the following:

"Have you ever wanted to be someone else? Maybe a math whiz, a superhero, the center on the basketball team, President of the United States, or even a nerd? Well, now is your chance. Anyone is possible, even one from outer space or someone who lived hundreds of years ago. I'll give you five minutes to write down at least five characters you might like to be. However, there are three things you must consider:

• Your parents must approve of this character.

• Your character must be appropriate for a school setting.

• Your character must be fictitious. No living person can be used."

After five minutes, have them share their ideas in groups of three, getting feedback. Then pass out the Analysis for Building Your Own Character sheet, and let them have the rest of the class time to fill out the form. There will not be enough time to finish, so they are to take it home and bring it back completed the next day.

Day 2: Writing Monologue Based on Analysis for Building Your Own Character

The students, having brought back their completed analysis, now take out another sheet of clean paper and, based on their analysis sheet, write a two-minute long monologue based on their analysis. Obviously, they cannot include everything on their analysis, so they have to choose what they think would be the most interesting thing to tell. They might want to think of it as a small autobiography.

They also have to consider to whom their character is talking. Is it a group of people such as your class? Or is it someone special? If it is someone special, who is this person and why are they talking to him or her. *Remind them they are to write in first person.* Give them twenty minutes to work.

Now have the class, as a group, read their pieces out loud so you can time them. You might want to do this several times, prompting them as they read. They need to think of how their characters stand and what kind of voices their characters use. *Remind them, too, they are their characters, not themselves.*

Most will have written enough to cover a minute. Let them work individually for the rest of the hour. Just before they are to leave, have them put the name of their character on the top of the paper, scratching out their name if they have put it anywhere on the monologue. Collect *all* papers, including the analysis, even if the students haven't completed their assignment.

Day 3: Reviewing or Continue Working on Monologue

Pass back the monologues and the analysis and give the students class time to review and/or finish their writing. Next, they need to rewrite their piece on a clean sheet of paper, double-spaced, with the name of their character on top. *Their real name is not to be anywhere on the paper.*

At the end of the period, collect all the papers. Explain that tomorrow they are going to become their characters for the entire hour. You will give them five minutes to change clothes at the beginning of class and time at the end to change back. Remind them that even if their character is older, they are still attending your drama class. The important thing is to remain in character for the entire class period, no giggling or breaking character.

Day 4: Presentation Day

After giving them time to change, have them go outside your door, as if they were just coming to class. Say "ring" to indicate the bell and then as they enter tell them to take a seat.

After everyone is seated, welcome them to class and say they need to get to know their fellow classmates, so you will call on them, using the monologues they had written. Before class, I made sure I had mixed up the order of the papers.

Select the first monologue and call out the name at the top. That character then comes up to the front of the room, reads his or her piece, and then asks if there are any questions. The students, as their characters, ask the presenter any questions not covered in the monologue. Allow this for one to two minutes, depending on your class size, then call up the next character, etc.

    I always notified the principal of this
    assignment, because on several occasions my
    students decided to be "tough customers" and had
    to be sent to the principal's office!

Below is a portion of one of the student monologues featuring Fearless Freddy.

> As I launched my vehicle into full gear, I could hear my wheels peel out. The wind rushed in my face and I felt free. I was *the* baddest dude on hot wheels this side of Whitaker Street. I had a gang and we terrorized the streets on our plastic hot wheels. Leather was replaced with sweats and He-Man T-shirts. I was soooo cool.
>
> I did life-threatening chicken races at speeds exceeding two miles an hour. I lived on the edge. The best was when I brought candy cigarettes and we all smoked, as we cruised the driveway looking for action. I didn't do any of the messy things like the Hell's Angels that cruised for babes. Instead I chased girls down yelling, "Cooties — Cooties." Oh, I was a real man!

Make sure there is enough time at the end of class for the students to change back into their clothes. Say "ring" again and they "leave" class.

The day after the presentation we always spent at least ten minutes debriefing, sometimes more.

Evaluation

The analysis is one grade, and the day they presented was another grade. Everyone generally got the same grade on the presentation day if they remained in character for the entire hour. I did not grade the actual monologue, but you certainly could.

Unit 8
Students Writing Their Own Show

Doing a student-driven production can be rewarding, not just for the actors but also for their parents, the school, and the community. It shows students can write, have ideas worth sharing, and take pride in their accomplishments. It can be done as a classroom production for the public, which is how I used it, or a production in the year's play schedule.

No Technical Aspects

This kind of play requires time to create, but does not need any special technical expertise. In addition, there are no scripts to buy or royalties to pay. It can be performed on a stage, in a gym, or even a large classroom. The trick is to make your actors seen and to change the audience's focus when a different speaker or group begins to perform.

Time Limit

There needs to be a time limit. You never want the entire show to be longer than ninety minutes. An audience will get restless and uninterested if the show is longer. More than ninety minutes listening to teenagers, or any age group for that matter, whether funny or sad, is enough. You will be running it with no intermission. No piece should be longer than three minutes, unless it is a duo. Then the time can change, possibly four to five minutes.

Writing the Show

Vary the Pieces

Start the process by having each student write a variety of six to eight pieces approximately three minutes long. Always have them include:

- One piece or more of poetry. Often poems can be divided among several students, if not the entire cast or class.
- Several pieces having at least two or more people. An audience can become quite bored if all the scenes are solos.
- Possibly a song or pantomime.

Collect each piece after it has been presented and keep it in a file. Students have a tendency to either lose their work and/or try to bluff their way through it, not having it written down.

Subject Ideas

What are the subjects? You can select a general topic such as Teenage Years or A Night of Firsts, for example, and write specific entries. I always tried to pick subjects students were interested in. Below is a list of topics I used over a ten-year period.

- "Firsts": day at school, day you drove the car, amusement park ride, etc.
- Advice to incoming freshman
- Being a freshman
- Best class
- Best friends or what a friend is
- Best or worst Christmas or birthday
- Birth or childhood
- Boyfriend or girlfriend
- Brothers or sisters
- Cheating
- Cooperation
- Death
- Extracurricular activities
- First big trip
- First crush
- Friends/friendship
- Job
- Junior or senior year
- Love
- Middle School
- Most embarrassing moment
- Most influential adult
- Most interesting or unique character you've ever met
- Most memorable day
- Most unforgettable teacher
- Most vivid childhood memory
- New brother or sister or stepfamily
- Parents or teachers

- Peer pressure
- Problems
- Prom or school dances
- Stress
- Talking on cell phones
- Tardies
- Texting
- What is acting?
- Who am I?
- Why drama or theatre?
- Worst experience
- Your hero

You will need six to eight days to complete this part of the production, as each piece will be presented one time to the entire class, either in one rehearsal or class period.

Musical Statue

After your students have written several pieces, take time to go back to the game of Statue, but with some additions. It is not only a great warm-up, but it teaches invention and introduces the idea of creating story from movement rather than the other way around.

Before class, you have made a playlist on an MP3 player or iPod containing short snippets of contrasting musical selections — at least fifteen or twenty of them. This takes a lot of time, but you only have to do it once, and you can find many uses for this list afterwards.

Divide your class into groups of four to six. There is only one real "rule" at the beginning:

- Whenever the music is playing, your students are moving; whenever it stops, they freeze.

Select one of your groups. Play a snippet of music, encouraging this group to move the way the music sounds. "Be free! Jump, move arms, skip. Whatever the music says to you." Then stop the music. Stress the importance of freezing instantly when the music stops in whatever position they find themselves. Then have another group get up and repeat until all groups have had a chance to hear the music and freeze.

After your students have gotten the hang of it, add an additional "rule":

- Beginning with the original group, after the music has stopped and everyone has frozen, say "go!" Each student launches immediately into a spontaneous improvisation, suggested by the position in which he or she is frozen. This will only last about thirty seconds.

You will probably have to yell "stop!" or have a whistle as it will be noisy. Then have the next groups come up, start the next piece of music, and once again the students move to the music, freeze when the music stops, and then improv. Be sure each group has a chance to try this. You may have to coach to make sure your students are really letting their body position suggest their improvisations.

Again, start with the first group, but this time add rule three:

- After they have moved and froze in place, give them a suggestion from one of the topics listed above under Subject Ideas. Your students are to improvise a real scene, based on your suggestion, with another person in their group.

Again, be sure that each group has a chance to participate, and, of course, with different music and topics.

A great way to end this activity is to do one large improv involving each student in the group or class.

When everyone has completed the activity, discuss the way the music enhanced the exercise. It created more varied movement. Without the music, and the differences in the music, all of the freezes would tend to be similar, and thus the improvisations would lack variety. A great question to ask is, "Why does music have so much emotional content?"

As they begin writing more of their pieces, have them keep this exercise in mind and the possibility of using a piece of music to best describe what they are writing about.

Selection Process

After all the pieces have been written and presented, the selection process begins. Keep in mind you want variety not only with content but also with solos, duos, and groups. Have each student choose two of their own pieces and rewrite them. Yes, rewriting is a must. Have them present their pieces again. This should take another two days.

Before the class as a whole or the cast selects the final pieces, there are several things to consider:

- Make sure your show is not maudlin. High school students love to write tearjerkers. Several serious pieces are certainly necessary, but an audience, I repeat, does not want to be assaulted by high school angst.
- Find out if any students have special talents: playing guitar, dancing, performing magic, etc. There is nothing wrong with showcasing these talents. It makes for a much more interesting evening of theatre. If music is involved, possibly one of the pieces could be incorporated into a song and/or dance, something the whole class or cast can participate in.
- Keep in mind the length of your show. Remember, you will need an opening number, discussed below. Also consider the audience reactions and the time for connecting the show together, also discussed below.
- Everyone in the class or cast will perform at least one piece, not necessarily their own. Be sure to remember you will not have an intermission. You want the show to last no longer than ninety minutes.

During the selection process it is possible a student will have two of his or her pieces chosen and another student will not have any picked. This is a cast or class decision. It may require a secret ballot. When the final pieces have been selected, you need to decide which student does which piece. It is not necessary for a student to do his or her own piece, but, I repeat, each student must perform at least one piece.

Three Samples of Student's Writing

Mrs. Klug

Yes, as I think back, I can remember her well, very well. It was freshman year. My older brother had given me a short orientation before school that day on what I should expect. He told me that the day would be very boring. I'd get some books, hear the same list of rules repeated seven times, then I'd go home. He told me that most of the teachers were pretty cool. Well, except for … Mrs. Klug, freshman English. Even kids who had never had Mrs. Klug would cringe at the sound of her name. But, I decided not to worry about it because I thought that he was just trying to scare me.

I got to school and my homeroom teacher gave me my schedule for first semester. I looked down the list until I came to 7th period, English I, teacher, Mrs. Klug. Some kid leaned over my shoulder, looked at my schedule, and said, "You're so stewed." My hands went clammy, my throat went dry, and I went through the whole day on the verge of vomiting.

Although it seemed like forever, 7th period came around and I slowly made my way to Mrs. Klug's room. No one was in the room. So I took a seat in the rear and sat quietly. The rest of the class slowly filled up the room and Mrs. Klug was nowhere in sight. "All right," I thought, "maybe she had a heart attack in the bathroom and we'll get a new teacher." But, no such luck. I heard the sound of footsteps approaching our room. I looked up and there she was standing in the doorway, staring right at ME! She had deep red eyes, hair up in a bun, dressed all in black! She stood there for at least five minutes, looking at each student individually, but saying nothing. I felt that something had to be done, so with all the courage that my body possessed I blurted out, "Good afternoon, Mrs. Klug!" She turned to me with her dark red eyes and stared at me for what seemed to be an eternity. Then she said, "Good afternoon Sam." Her voice was soft and kind, not like I had imagined.

She walked to her desk and began reading through her class roster. When she came to my name she looked up and smiled right at me. I smiled back thinking, "This year may not be so bad after all."

Problem Solving

Life is filled with problems.
Some big, some little.
It's just filled with problems.
So how do you go about solving a problem?
The troubling thing about problem solving is how to go about it.
Some people try to walk around their problems, others just ignore them.

This works sometimes, but sometimes a problem just can't be forgotten.

It pinches you everywhere you go.

With a problem like this the first step in solving it is to survey the situation.

Feel around; get a good handle on exactly what's wrong.

Then find a way to work it out.

If that doesn't work, it is time to resort to the final method of problem solving.

Dive right in!

Don't be afraid to dig right in and get your hands dirty.

In the end you will be glad you did.

The Plain Girl

Usually clumsy, not sure of herself: The girl steps out onto the huge expanse of stage. She feels its life, the numerous characters that have walked here before. They all speak to her, and she feeds off the energy they give. As her mouth opens, and her body moves, she is able to escape, no longer feeling her own insecurities.

The character that speaks and moves through her engulfs her, and she can be beautiful or ugly, old or young, strong or weak, alive or dead on that stage. In her mind she is that player in the script. The character, no longer one-dimensional, but made real and whole with the life breathed into her by this plain girl.

On the stage she escapes her own life. She becomes another, and lives in another world. The audience responds, and she feels their tangible, immense energy. But, the illusion ends as the girl steps off the stage.

Yet the power to make people laugh, cry, love, hate, wonder, and applaud all lie within her. The stage feels like home to her, a place to live out the lives of characters born through this plain, insecure girl.

Acting is something I've always loved. I realized early what a wonderful feeling it is to become someone else, and to captivate the audience making them feel the emotions you choose. Theater has taught me a great deal about the escape that can be made when one steps onto the stage. I love drama. It allowed me to escape my own life, and become someone else, someone real. I've grown as a person, in my portrayal of all the characters I have encountered, for they all possessed some aspect of me.

```
    See three of my students performing during our
presentation  to  the  public  on  my  website
margaretfjohnson.com.  Under  Photos,  click  on
"Bits and Pieces."
```

Opening Number

Next you need to consider the opening of the show. Three are listed below.

Poem

You could start with a poem in the form of a cadence written by students. Below is the one we did my last year of teaching. The students marched in from the back of the auditorium, lined up in all the aisles, and shouted it out. When it was over, the students entered the acting area and the actual show began.

Attention
About face
March
Hup 2-3-4
Give it up 2-3-4
Hup 2-3-4
We're the fighting Spartan team
In drama this is what we've gleaned
Attendance is a do or die
If you don't show, your play won't fly
No hats ... No gum
No hats ... No gum
No hat, no gum
Perform

If you do not know your lines
She will kick you in your behind
You will have to improvise

If you don't they'll hear your cries.
No hats … No gum
No hats … No gum
No hat, no gum
Yell loud
Practice is the key to success
Hopefully you won't have to undress
Take the class if you dare
Mrs. J. has purple hair
No hats … No gum
No hats … No gum
No hat, no gum
Stage left

Write down blocking in your book
If you don't you'll get the hook.
Getting applause really rocks.
Just like brand new fuzzy socks
No hats … No gum
No hats … No gum
No hat, no gum
Our plays

Improv quick, you know the drill
Don't act dumb and don't stand still.
Say good lines and don't say "no"
Whatever happens, you must go.
No hats … No gum
No hats … No gum
No hat, no gum
Right on

Just before we start our play
There's one more thing we have to say
Everybody have a real swell day
No hats … No gum
No hats … No gum

No hat, no gum
The end

Warm-Ups

If you do warm-ups both vocally and physically in your class or rehearsals, start the show with them. It is a great way to immediately involve the audience.

Tongue Twister

Using a tongue twister as your opening number grabs the audience's attention. It is fun for the audience and a great way to vocally warm up your actors for the show.

Selecting the Order of Acts and Tying it Together

Now comes the time to select the order of the pieces. You will want to intersperse not only subject matter, not everything serious or humorous put together, but you'll want the types of writing, duos or solos, intermingled. You want to start the show with one of your strongest pieces and, of course, end on a high note.

How they will be tied together? Here are three examples.

Music

Music is a natural. It gives the show energy. Let each student select his or her piece of music introducing his or her scene, no more than twenty to twenty-five seconds. This permits time for movement and changing focus.

Students Introduce Each Piece

Have a different student introduce each piece, which has been written beforehand, allowing each student to perform a piece and introduce another piece.

Write a Script

Use the various topics of the pieces to tie the "play" together. I found this the most difficult and only used it once. I think if you want to use this, you must have a knack for writing and/or a class or cast who jumps at the chance to write.

What's Left?

Title

Every show needs a title. I called our show "Bits and Pieces" because the evening was based on incidents from my students' lives.

Rehearsal

Rehearsals can be any length you require. I usually took four days.

Program

Every show also needs a program. It does not have to be fancy or take much time to create. The names of the students and the title of their piece are all that is required. More can be added, of course. It can be done on one sheet of colored paper and makes a great place to advertise your fall production. I have included our last program in the Appendix on page 167.

Performance

Depending on how you have this show scheduled in your year, it can run for one to three days or nights. Our show became a tradition in early October. Since we would be doing our fall production in several weeks, we did not charge and only ran one night.

Evaluation

I would give a blanket grade for each piece the students wrote, a little higher grade for the rewrite, then a blanket grade for the performance. I did not feel I could give anything but blanket grades this early in the semester or year. I wanted my students to feel comfortable with performing, not worrying about grades.

A Final Note or Two

As you are winding up your semester or year, there are two things you need to consider if you want your drama department to grow. In this time of drastic educational cuts, the arts are taking a beating. We know how important they are — they enrich our lives — and most of our students would agree as well, but the general public is not always aware of their importance.

Eight Grade Handout

You need to contact your local middle schools in your area letting those incoming freshman know about your drama program and the classes they can take. Counselors generally do not effectively promote the drama program. I am not in any way saying counselors are not doing their jobs, but they are much more concerned with the basics than the fine arts, so you need to "toot your own horn."

Creating a handout and/or presenting a "show" are two ways of doing this I found effective. Clearing any handouts or presentations must be done with the principal. Most are more than willing to let you notify their graduating eighth graders. I used the Handout for Incoming Eighth Graders in the Appendix on page 169. I ran it on colored paper, formatted it differently, had two handouts per page, and used a little clip art to jazz it up.

End of Year Letter Home

I have to honestly admit that during my years of teaching, I never truly appreciated the support I received from my administration as well as my parents. I guess I just expected the drama department to remain strong year after year and the parents to support not only our drama department but our school mill levies as well.

As I was reviewing my last fifteen years of teaching, I came across a letter I wrote to my Drama 2 parents in the mid 90s. I had had an exceptionally great advanced drama class and wanted the parents to know how much I appreciated their kids. This got me to thinking, "Wasn't each year's classes exceptional in some way? Why didn't I write the parents each year? Why hadn't I thanked them for their support?" Yes, of course, it takes time, but it is time well spent.

In this age of computers, the trick is to make it personal. Take the time to print it out, sign it, and send it by mail, not email. *Please.* Every parent loves to hear how special their child is and this is just another way of enforcing that strong positive bond between school and home. See the End of Year Letter to Parents in the Appendix page 171.

Teaching theatre is not unlike what it takes to make a great life: caring for others, accepting each other for who we are, being responsible and dependable, but most important of all, being proud of what we do. I hope you have had a great time working with your students on these various activities, exercises, handouts, lessons, and techniques for the drama classroom. Since retiring I have to say that a day doesn't go by that I don't miss my kids and the wonderful times I had in Room 155 at Sentinel High School.

If you are also the play director in your school, be sure to look for my other book, *The Drama Teacher's Survival Guide*. Also check out my website: margaretfjohnson.com and my blog:

http://contemporarydramanewsletter.contemporarydrama.com/public/blog/203097

Appendix

Critique Formats

Your Name

Name of Play

Date you attended the show

Basic Critique Form

1st paragraph: Write a two-sentence summary of the play. If there is a subplot, write a two-sentence summary of it. Start your sentence: The (Title of Play) is about ...

2nd paragraph: State the theme of the play. This is the author's purpose and/or message. Relate this theme to the characters and action of the play. Don't just say, "Crime doesn't pay." Tell me how in this production it didn't pay. Site specific things that will prove your point.

3rd paragraph: This paragraph discusses two areas of technical theatre. Pick one: set, costumes, or lights and pick one: program, tickets, or poster. Tell how each related to the play. Remember the points in the Technical Theatre Packet. Use details from the play to support your discussion.

4th paragraph: Take one lead character and analyze how the actor or actress made you believe in that character. What personality traits, voice, and action did he or she use? Did you believe him or her? Why or why not? Give details. This is *not* an analysis of the character, but the actor's portrayal of the character.

5th paragraph: Give your opinion or feeling of the play. Explain, using examples from the play. Be specific!

Acting Format

1st paragraph: Who is your character and what does he or she do in the play? What motivates him or her to do what he or she does in the play?

2nd paragraph: What did you as an actor or actress do to create your role? Why did you make those choices and what influenced you to make them?

3rd paragraph: What were your best and worst performances and why?

4th paragraph: Discuss how everyone made the performance successful.

5th paragraph: What did you learn from this performance?

Crew Format

1st paragraph: Discuss your job and the hours involved with this technical activity.

2nd paragraph: Discuss your process of developing you crew work: how this changed or stayed the same, what you had to do to get the job done, etc.

3rd paragraph: Discuss how your involvement with the show enhanced the production.

4th paragraph: Discuss how everyone in the production, actors too, made the production successful.

5th paragraph: What one thing have you learned from this production that will enhance your next production?

Children's Theatre Format

1st paragraph: Write a two-sentence summary of the play. If there is a subplot, write a two-sentence summary of it.

2nd paragraph: What was the moral of the play? Be sure to relate it to the characters and action of the play. Be specific.

3rd and 4th paragraphs: The ingredients for children's theatre are as follows: music, dance, action, color, and interesting, but not too scary, characters. Pick two of them, one for each paragraph, explaining why each is important and if this production made both work. Again, give details.

5th paragraph: Pick one of the characters you liked most and tell why. What did the actor or actress do to create their role? What choices did they make to create this believable character?

Dance Format

1st paragraph: Pick one of the dance numbers. Could the audience relate the title of the dance to the actual performance? Example: if the name of a particular dance number is "Angry Sea," could you, as a member of the audience, actually tell that the dancers were portraying an angry sea?

2nd paragraph: Select several other dances. What effect did costuming have on the different dances? Were the dances and costumes related?

3rd paragraph: Select several more dances. What part did music and lighting play in the various dance numbers? How effective were they?

4th paragraph: Choreography is defined as the art of composing dances while directing is putting the important pieces of a play (people, words, action, etc.) together in front of an audience. What aspects of theatre must the choreographer of a dance and the director of a play be aware of and have in common?

5th paragraph: Sets and props are an important part of theatre. What roles do they play on a dance stage? Are they necessary? Why or why not?

Letter to Drama 1 Parents

Dear Parents,

Welcome to Sentinel's wonderful world of Drama. As we start a brand new semester, I would like to let you know what is happening in Drama 1. As we have no textbook in this class, all assignments are to be put in a notebook, which will be graded several times during the semester. It will include the following: Drama 1 Course Management and Content, Grade Sheet, Productions Around Missoula, Basic Critique Format, the packet we're working on, critiques, and all daily work along with paper and pen. This notebook must be in class every day and can be considered part of the daily grade.

ATTENDANCE — Absences, as well as tardies, will be handled according to Sentinel's Policy. Make up on work missed during absences is the sole responsibility of the student. Students must make every effort to be here. As this class is group-oriented with mostly IN CLASS ACTIVITIES, when they are absent, group work and discussion is missed, which will be very difficult to make up. If students are going to miss class due to a SCHOOL ACTIVITY (science, music, athletic, or other trip), they MUST turn in assignments BEFORE they leave, receive assignments for the next day, and come the following day, ready for class, assignments done. This rule is also in effect if students are absent from school for just a portion of the day, including the period that Drama 1 meets. I am here every day after school, as well as lunch on Thursday, for anyone who needs to check grades, check assignments, or get help. Absences can also affect other students' grades. Everyone in this class depends on each other. Continued absences can affect their grade.

MID-QUARTER PROGRESS REPORT — At mid-quarter time, you will be notified on your child's progress in class with a mid-quarter report. This report is to be taken home, signed by you, and returned to me for credit.

DAILY WORK 46% — Students do not and will not be excused from class to go to their locker for pen, paper, notebook, etc. They are expected to bring to class what is required at all times. A variety of subjects will be covered this semester including: Acting, Choral Reading, Class Plays, Improvisation, Pantomime, and Technical Theatre. 90% of the daily work in this class is oral, performed in front of the class.

PLAY CRITIQUE 15% — Each student must see three plays for the semester: one performance of a play outside of Sentinel plus seeing two Sentinel plays are required. A specific written critique form will be handed out and discussed in detail before students have to write. This written review is due the Monday after the last performance of the play. If this should cause a financial hardship, have your child see me.

TESTS AND QUIZZES 6% — There will be two written tests covering Technical Theatre during the semester worth 110 points. Several quizzes will be given during the semester over information I feel is important. It is generally over material handed out for overnight reading.

FINAL PERFORMANCE 33% — This presentation includes almost everything that has been covered in the semester (choral reading, mime, improv, plays, etc.). It will be performed in the Little Theatre the last week of the semester in the evening for the public, free of charge.

TWO FINAL NOTES
- All work is due WHEN it is called for, usually at the beginning of the class period.
- The majority of each student's grade is determined by the IMAGINATIVE AND CREATIVE way in which the student's work is done.

Letter to Drama 2 Parents

Dear Parents,

Welcome to Sentinel's wonderful world of theatre. As we start a brand new year, I would like to take a couple of minutes to let you know what I expect and what we're doing in Drama 2.

Margaret F. Johnson

NOTEBOOK

There is no textbook for this class. All assignments including analyses, corrected critiques, daily assignment sheets, and calendars as well as scripts are to be put in a notebook along with paper and pen. This notebook must be in class every day and can be considered part of daily work. All the items mentioned below are included in the Course Management and Content booklet, which is also in their notebooks.

ATTENDANCE

(25% of Quarter Grade)

Students must make every effort to be in class every day as this class is TOTALLY group oriented with IN CLASS ACTIVITIES. When students are absent, group work and discussion is missed, which will be very difficult to make up. An absence also affects others' grades. Everyone in this class depends on everyone else. If students are going to miss class due to a SCHOOL ACTIVITY (science, music, athletic, or other trip), they MUST turn in assignments BEFORE they leave, and receive assignments for the next day. On their return, they'll be ready for class, assignments done. THIS RULE IS ALSO IN EFFECT IF they are absent from school for just a portion of the day, including the period Drama 2 meets. I am here every day after school as well as lunch on Thursday. Bringing treats to the whole class within two days of the violation can eliminate infractions such as tardies and wearing hats.

DAILY WORK

(42% of Quarter Grade)

Daily work is divided into two sections: written (including analyses, critiques, and creative compositions) and oral (including tryouts, memorization, doing improv, etc.).

PRODUCTION WORK

(33% of Quarter Grade)

The majority of this class will be spent creating FOUR productions. The titles and dates will depend on the class. Each student will have the opportunity to act in these shows, as well as do all the technical aspects: lighting, costumes, props, set, publicity, makeup, and directing.

1. October 18: *BITS & PIECES*. A show written by the students
2. Nov. 30th and Dec. 1st: *2ND CLASS*
3. Sometime in March a fun musical
4. The last week of May: *A children's variety show for several grade schools around the Sentinel area*

I do not accept late work, written or otherwise. Work is due when called for.

Introduction Handout Group A

First name and why you were called that. (My dad was named after a cow!)

____

____

Your favorite movie, musical group, play, or TV program.

____

____

Your favorite color or food.

____

____

What was your first pet's name and what kind of pet was it?

____

____

What was your favorite children's book?

____

____

This famous line is from a movie or a play. Fill in words so the line makes sense. If you know the line, try not to fill in the correct word. Example: "Frankly my dear, I don't give a *turkey sandwich*."

To _______________ or not to _______________ that is the question ...

Introduction Handout Group B

First name and why you were called that. (I am named for my Grandmother Maggie.)

____

____

Your favorite color or food.

____

____

What was the name of your first pet and what kind of pet was it?

____

____

Are you a morning or night person?

____

____

This famous line is from a movie or a play. Fill in words so the line makes sense. If you know the line, do not fill in the correct word. Example: "Frankly my dear, I don't give a *turkey sandwich*."

Toto, I've got a _______________ we're not in _______________ anymore.

Improvisation Starters

You're sick. I'm telling Mom
Help me! I'm falling.
Shhhh. Did you hear that?
Trick or treat!
John? Tom? Pete?
I saw that! Stop it now!
There, there. Stop crying.
I'm scared. Help me.
Today's my birthday.
What's that you're eating? Bugs?
I hate your guts.
A shark! Run for your lives.
Haven't I seen you somewhere before?
Gotcha! Third time's the best!
Is this your house?
This is for you. Congrats.
Answer the door. *Now!*
There's something in my eye.
Stand up. It's now your turn.
I'm blind. What did you do?
Catch.
Who was that man?
Close your eyes. You're it!
Have you seen my kitty? He ran away last night.
Where's my teddy bear? You stole it!
It's empty. Where did you put it?
Next! Finally!
Oh no! The baby's coming!

Technical Packet

Tech Terms

Like many other trades and occupations, the theatre has its own colorful language. Note these:

Above: Upstage of (as in the direction, "Cross behind or above the sofa").

Ad-lib: To extemporize during a performance.

Amateur: One who works in the theatre without pay.

Apron: The part of stage projecting in front of curtain.

Aside: Line to audience or other character, not noticed by other characters onstage.

Backstage: Portion of theatre not included in auditorium and stage proper.

Batten: Movable pipe above the stage, used for hanging scenery.

Below: Downstage of (as in "Cross in front or below the sofa").

Blank: Mental fade-out causing lines or business to be forgotten.

Blocking: Putting actions to the words in the script.

Bomb: Theatrical dud.

Book: Play manuscript.

Booking: To hire companies or actors.

Borderlight: Strips of reflector spotlights in a metal container.

Build: To bring a scene to a climax by increasing volume, emphasis, pace, or intensity.

Burlesque: Exaggerated acting, often referred to as "ham."

Business: Stage action.

Call: Warning to actors to be ready for entrance.

Callboard: Bulletin board backstage on which are posted important notices for actors and crews.

Cattle call: The type of audition at which many actors are present. It is open to anyone.

Catwalk: Ledge near overhead lights, used by electricians.

Chorus: Group of singers, dancers, or speakers working in unison.

Civic/Community Theatre: Noncommercial Theatre.

Clear stage: The command to leave stage.

Close in: Move closer together.

Close the cues: Shorten time spaces between the end of one character's line and the following lines; pickup tempo. Also *pickup cues*.

Come down: Approach part of stage nearer audience.

Counter: As one actor moves, another actor shifts his or her position in the opposite direction so everyone can be seen and no one is standing in front of anyone.

Cover: To attempt to hide mistakes in lines or action. Also, to block another character from audience's view.

Crepe hair: Wool-like substance used for making beards.

Cross: Actor's movement from one part of stage to another abbreviated by writing "X."

Cue: Last words of a speech, signaling another to speak or enter.

Cue sheet: List of cues for stage noises and light changes.

Curtain going up: The signal to the cast that the scene is ready to begin.

Curtain line: Imaginary line where front curtain hangs between the audience and stage. Also, last line of play.

Cyc/Cyclorama: A white or blue tautly stretched canvas drop or plaster dome across the back wall of the stage, which when lit simulates the sky.

Director: One who oversees and orchestrates the mounting of a theatre production by unifying all aspects of production. He or she also tells actors where to move when giving their lines.

Downstage: Toward the audience.

Drop: A flat piece of fabric, generally painted, hung from a batten that forms part of the scenery.

Fake: To seem to be doing something without doing it.

Flats: Pieces of scenery consisting of a wood frame covered with canvas, muslin, or a hard surface used for walls.

Flies: Space directly above the stage into which scenery is raised.

Flop: Theatre production that fails.

Focus: To center attention on something.

Fourth wall: Imaginary wall filling in the proscenium arch through which the audience can see in and observe the action of the play.

Give stage: Move to less important position.

Green room: Lounge near stage used by actors, crew, and director.

Grips: Stagehands.

Ground cloth: Large canvas covering floor or acting areas to muffle footsteps.

Ground row: Low flats set on stage floor for scenic background; generally used as bushes or grass. It can also be used to give the illusion of depth.

Grouping: Arranging characters for meaningful, emotional, and best interests of the play.

Gypsy: A dancer who goes from musical show to musical show, often in the chorus.

Hand props: Items that actors carry onstage for business.

Hold: Keep position without moving.

House: Audience.

In the red: Losing money on the show.

Interview audition: Private audition, opposite of cattle call.

Jury: First-night audience.

Improvisation: Short bit with lines and action created by actor. Often used as rehearsal exercise.

Improvise: Unprepared lines and action; often needed to cover for something unforeseen in the actual running of a show.

Kill: To eliminate a piece of scenery or property from set, or to black out the lights.

Levels: Acting areas placed higher than stage level with the use of platforms, which are at different heights.

Lines: Speeches of play.

Milk it dry: (Slang) Squeeze the most laughs from line or expression.

Monologue: Speech by one person.

Notices: Reviews, clippings, dramatic criticism.

Off-Stage: Area of the stage not enclosed by set; not visible to the audience.

On-Stage: Portion of stage enclosed by set and visible to audience.

Open up: Turn more toward audience.

Out front: Area occupied by audience.

Overlap: Picking up cue before previous speaker has finished.

Pace: Timing of lines and action.

Papering the house: Filling the theatre for a performance with friendly reviewers.

Panning: Unfavorable reviewing.

Pit: Orchestra area, generally in front of the apron in modern theatres.

Pickup cues: To begin speaking immediately on the last word of the previous speaker's lines, or attach your line to the former speech, no space between.

Places: Signal for actors to begin their scene.

Plant: 1.) Person stationed in audience who has function in play. 2.) Line, idea, or character that significantly foreshadows some important element coming later in play.

Point-up or Point-to: Emphasize or play-up idea or character.

Position: Actor's place onstage as set by director.

Prompt book or prompt script: Script marked with directions and cues to be used by stage manager or assistant director.

Properties (props): All objects onstage exclusive of scenery.

Rake: Gradual slope of floor, i.e. raked house or raked stage.

Ramp: Sloping walk leading to higher elevation.

Revamp: To rewrite scene or play by bringing it up to date.

Revolving stage: Turntable stage.

Run: Length of the play's engagement.

Run-Through: To rehearse a play without stopping.

Scene: Division within an act; usually refers to short section where there is a change of characters.

Shtick: (Slang) Bits of cliché character business designed to get laughs. (David Letterman's "Top Ten.")

Script: Typewritten or printed copy of play.

Shoestring production: Putting on a play with a minimum of financial expenditure.

Sides: Pages of the manuscript holding an actor's lines and cues, usually only used in musicals. It is not the whole play.

Sitting on their hands: (Slang) An unresponsive audience.

SRO: Standing room only.

Stage call: Meeting of cast and director onstage for instructions.

Stage directions: Instructions in script of play or the movements a director gives an actor when an actor speaks.

Stage hands: Helpers employed backstage — in the movies called a *grip*.

Stage left: Actor's left when facing audience.

Stage manager: Person responsible for play in production, calls cues for actors, lights, sound, set changes.

Stage right: Actor's right when facing audience.

Stage superstitions:

Bad luck:

1. Being wished good luck.
2. Whistling in dressing room.
3. Using old rabbit's foot for new makeup.
4. Opening telegrams before first performance.

Good luck:

1. Pocketful of coins.
2. Cat backstage.
3. Wearing old shoes associated with hit.
4. Wishing player bad luck — "Break a leg."

Stage whisper: Speaking just loud enough for audience to hear, but gives the illusion of whispering.

Steal a scene: To call attention to yourself when it should be elsewhere.

Strike: Call given to stage crew to remove scenery and props or dismantle the entire production.

Tableau: Living picture (people frozen like statues).

Tag: Line at climax (pointing up preceding speech).

Take a call: Bow before audience.

Take stage: Move into stronger stage position.

Teaser: Overhead drapery used to mask lighting equipment.

"Tech" director: Person responsible for all production crews.

The road: Area outside New York played by touring companies.

The sticks: Small towns played by touring companies.

Topping cues: Pick up the energy, the pace, and the volume of a scene; one actor jumps on top of a previous character's line thereby building tension and emotional impact.

Tormentor: Flats or drapes at sides, upstage of act curtain, used to mask backstage.

Trap: Opening in stage floor.

Turkey: Theatrical flop or "bomb."

Turn in or turn out: Turn your body toward or away from others.

Upstage: Toward the back of the stage.

Upstaging: Moving upstage to gain audience's attention, thus compelling cast to turn toward that actor, thus facing away from the audience.

Wardrobe: Costumes and articles of dress for production.

Wings: Space at either side of stage, behind the scene, or offstage.

X: Abbreviation for "cross," as in XDL is "cross down left."

The terms listed below have to do with actors, their parts, and the type of plays they would be in.

Dramatis personae: Latin, meaning persons in the play.

Bit part: Role with very few lines, if any, and/or little action.

Character part: Role depicting unusual individual.

Ensemble: Group of players acting together.

Equity: Actors' Equity Association, an actors' union.

Featured: Billing secondary only to the star role.

Ham: Actor who is bad, but thinks he is good.

Headliner: Star or leading player.

Heavy: Usually villain of cast or adult in serious role.

Ingénue: Young girl playing love interest.

Juvenile: Player of youthful roles.

Lead: Actor playing the most prominent or important part.

Masque: Early dramatic presentation of mythology.

Quick study: One who can memorize a part quickly.

Repertory: Collection of plays that may be readily performed because of familiarity to actors.

Rep show: Company playing repertory.

Revue: Musical comedy, without plot.

Stock: Company performing a new play every week.

Trouper: Seasoned actor who always works for play's best interest.

Understudy: Actor capable of playing another's role in an emergency.

Walk-On: Minor role with few lines.

U=Up   C=Center   D=Down

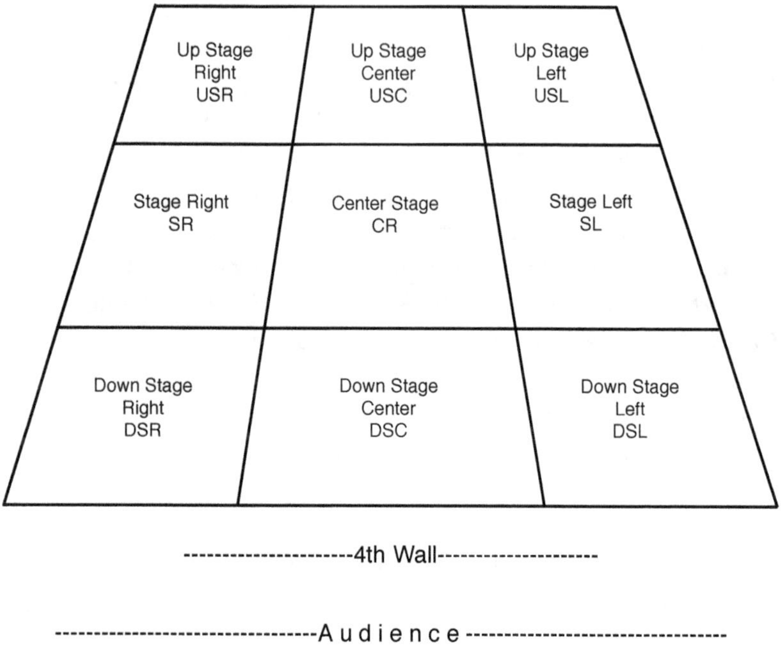

Up Stage Right USR	Up Stage Center USC	Up Stage Left USL
Stage Right SR	Center Stage CR	Stage Left SL
Down Stage Right DSR	Down Stage Center DSC	Down Stage Left DSL

----------------------4th Wall---------------------

--------------------------------A u d i e n c e----------------------------------

Important Areas of Theatre Production

Three Types of Theatres

Theatre in the Round or Arena

This was the first type of theatre. It originated during the first great period of drama in Greece approximately 500 B.C. It was held outside and resembled a football field, the actors in the field and the audience up in the stands watching. There was no actual theatre. They used a natural amphitheater with the audience sitting on the hill, above the actors, with the actors acting at the base. It became obvious that the actors needed to have excellent voices to project in such an area as well as costumes created to make them seem larger. Each actor wore a headdress, tall stilt-like shoes, a mask that helped project his voice, and padded costumes, all which made him seem larger than life.

Today this theatre is called intimate theatre because the audience, unlike their Greek counterparts, is close to the actors. The audience usually surrounds the acting area. Most plays successfully done with this type of theatre are those with relatively small casts.

Thrust Stage

During the second great period of drama, in the late 1500s, generally called The Elizabethan Era after Queen Elizabeth I, Shakespeare performed his plays in a horseshoe-shaped theatre building called "The Wooden O." The stage was at one end of a building and the audience surrounded the stage on three sides. Part of the front of the stage stuck out into the audience or *thrust* out. This type of theatre combined proscenium and arena. Today the most popular use of the thrust stage is the Guthrie Theatre in Minneapolis, Minnesota.

Proscenium

During the 1870s the audience dictated to the playwrights and actors that they were tired of seeing fake scenery, shallow personalities, and unbelievable situations. They wanted to see *real life* on the stage, to see real people, like them. They wanted to suffer and celebrate with the characters portrayed on the stage. They wanted to believe that there was a real house onstage, with running water, etc., giving birth to the *Realistic Movement.*

With this came the advent of the Proscenium or Picture Frame Theatre. When you walk into most theatres, or even movie houses, what do you see? The proscenium wall, which takes its name from the proskenion of the Greek theatre, separates the auditorium from the stage.

When the audience sits in the auditorium, they are facing a wall with a hole cut out of it. This opening, whatever its size, is called the proscenium arch. Within that arch the lives of people are presented, in their homes, offices, or wherever. The audience is a "peeping Tom" spying on the actors who go on living their lives with hate, fear, and love, unaware of the audience. This Picture Frame or arch creates a fourth wall where the act curtain closes and opens. If actors step beyond that imaginary line where the curtain has drawn, they are *breaking the fourth wall.*

As the years progressed, an addition, called an apron, was made to the front of the stage. This allowed the actors to get closer to the audience and communicate with them, as in the arena theatre.

An interesting sidelight of the Realistic Period was the introduction of the director. Until this time, one of the actors was the director, but with realism one person was needed to look at everyone and see if they were real — thus the director.

Factors in Play Selection

The choice of play is the first important duty of any director.

Literary Worth

The foremost questions directors should ask are, "Is the play worth doing? Does it have substance (a message or moral), is it well written, or is it a bit of nonsense that is just done for fun?" Not every play done in high school needs to be Shakespeare, but there must be something in the play worth spending six to eight weeks on. The play must challenge the actors, as well as the director.

Available Talent

The choice of a play is always affected by the number, gender, physical maturity, talent, and training of the actors and actresses available at any given time. There are few plays that cannot, at some time, be cast at a high school.

Facilities

Many high school stages have little or none of the following: fly loft, storage, and construction areas. This lack of facilities definitely affects the choice of plays. The size of the auditorium also has a great deal to do with play selection. If the theatre is small, modification will be needed if shows require large casts and/or many sets. A small theatre works well for intimate plays with small casts. If, on the other hand, the auditorium is large, possibly in a gymnasium, shows with large casts are possible. Bad acoustics, as well as scheduling rehearsals in the gymnasium or large auditorium, will often cause directors to eliminate certain plays from their play schedule. If a large cast is being considered and no costume or makeup room is available, directors might also eliminate that choice.

It is difficult to say whether or not any play can be done in a specific facility. How would you rate your theatre? What shows are good for your theatre? Why? Do you have any scheduling problems?

Production Costs

When any play is being considered, the cost of royalty (fee charged by publishers to present play) and scripts must be considered first. No play can be done without spending money on either of these. Most scripts cost between $6 and $8. Most royalty is $90 for the first performance and $40-$50 for any succeeding performances, unless you are doing a musical, which is much more expensive. Both of these items *must be paid in advance of the production!* So before we've had tryouts (auditions), how much money has been spent?

Costumes

This is the most important technical area of play production in the high school.

Purposes:

1. To clothe the actors.
2. To help establish the period of time in history, the time of year, and or the time of day.
3. To help distinguish one actor from another — character delineation.
4. To communicate the play.
5. To give the actors the physical feel of their characters — psychological effect on the actor.

Costuming is an integral part of the total stage picture. Each garment worn by the actor must make a statement about the production, as well as its character. For high school theatre, money being in very short supply, costumes become more important than set and lighting. So, where do these costumes come from?

Buying

Buying costumes is generally the most expensive way to costume a show. They may be purchased at any costume rental company. Other reasonable places to buy costumes are church rummage, estate, or neighborhood garage sales, the Salvation Army or Goodwill. Directors should search these sales with an eye for things that can be used again and again. They should especially be on the lookout for floor-length dresses of all kinds. These can be adapted to many different periods with the addition of new sleeves and trimmings. Formals, wedding gowns, bridesmaid's dresses, graduation gowns, and nightgowns are most useful.

Renting

Renting costumes from either the nearest college or university or the large costume rental firms is a great way of getting period costumes, even though there may be drawbacks. Generally, rented costumes are professionally made, of good quality, clean, and usually based upon authentic costumes of the period. They are also expensive, $50-$60 for one week per costume plus shipping charges, difficult to fit as they are not made for the specific actor, and must be returned after the last performance.

Borrowing

Every town or city is a storehouse of potential costumes. Family attics sometimes provide authentic period clothes, which can be adapted for the play. However, these garments are often precious and their material quite fragile. Caution should be taken when using them.

Another source is service clubs. Many of them have costumes from variety shows. Directors can also check with local merchants. Cleaners frequently have unclaimed clothing. Motels, doctors, offices, and restaurants can sometimes provide uniforms if their employees wear them. The local National Guard or V.F.W. might be able to assist with military uniforms. Also, check with the "lost and found" department of the school.

If costumes are borrowed, directors and costume crew should handle them with great care, as they can be easily torn and soiled. Having the items dry cleaned before returning them is a standard practice — be sure to check with the owner before anything is done. Any article borrowed should be returned in better condition than when it was borrowed. A thank you note should always be written.

Students Providing Own Costumes

A production that has the actors bring their own costumes is very inexpensive, but can be disastrous. A careful coordination is needed. This can be accomplished by having a coordinator, other than the director (a mother or fellow teacher), who will select those clothes that would work well for costumes. If the costumes are to be made by each student, this coordinator can select the patterns and material, and make detailed instructions of how to construct the costumes. This helps by:

- Making all costumes look unified.
- Making a statement about the play.
- Limiting how much each student can spend on his costume.

When producing *Macbeth,* a director left the job of costuming up to the individual student and his parent. There was no thought towards any production concept. As a result, Lady Macbeth was dressed in white satin and her husband in cheap cotton! What is wrong with that picture?

Making Costumes

This term is often called *building costumes.* The school purchases patterns and fabrics, measure their actors, and then makes all the costumes. This is the next most expensive way to provide costumes — buying patterns and material, as well as the time to make them. When costumes are specifically made for a production, under the guidance of the director, it has several advantages because they:

- Are made for a specific production.
- Fit the actors.
- Are absolutely correct for the show.

When the production is over, they can then be used again and again, becoming part of your stock costumes.

Stock Costumes

Stock costumes are costumes that are stored and used for many different productions. I used many costumes over and over again, with slight changes. Often directors will ask for clothing donations in their programs with "Your trash may be our treasure."

Lighting

Purposes:

- To illuminate the stage.
- To set a mood.
- To provide realistic effects like daylight, dawn, night.
- To create special effects like shadows, lightning, explosions.
- To substitute for or become the visual design, by using colors and gobos.

To provide colored lights onstage, gelatin (gel) is used. It is made of a non-flammable plastic, comes in a sheet, which covers approximately six lights, and is approximately $7.

The choice of lighting colors will depend on the mood of the play, the time of day, the season, and the apparent light source. Experimenting with colors is usually the way to obtain the desired effect. Colors of the costumes also play an important part in gel selection.

Most high schools have very limited lighting facilities. A six 2500-watt dimmer and automatic two preset dimmer board costs approximately $2,600. This does not include the special lighting, which runs at least $200 an instrument, $36 a light bulb or lamp, and $30 for C clamps, plug, and gel frame. The most important thing is that the actors be seen. If it just means to turn on the available lights that is fine.

Properties

Purposes:

- To help set a mood.
- To establish various locations.
- To assist the actors in portraying their roles.

Few props are truly essential for a production. I saw a production that required many, many props, and the decision was to mime all of them — it worked beautifully. All props should augment the production without detracting from its message.

There are four types of props:

- Decorative: Furniture or objects onstage that serve no practical purpose but help to give character to the setting.
- Floor: All the furniture normally used by the actors.
- Hand: Small objects carried to or from the stage by the actors or handled by them while onstage, such as a glass, book, dishes, or flowers.
- Costume: These props would be considered an accessory such as umbrellas, purses, gloves, or spectacles.

Makeup

Makeup is the final step in all actors' efforts to bring their characters to life.

Purposes:

- For illusion: Makeup helps to create the illusion of age, health, occupation, heredity, race, environment, and temperament.
- For revealing character: Makeup does not create the character, it only helps to reveal it. No makeup is complete without an actor underneath. A makeup that is conceived as a work in itself, unrelated to a specific performance or character, is worse than useless, even if it is a brilliant execution, because it will destroy the actor's characterization.
- For compensation: For the effects of stage lighting and the distance the actor is from the audience.

Makeup provides actors with valuable and often necessary help after they have done all that they can without it. Like speech and body movement, makeup is part of an actor's craft, and actors who neglect their makeup risk failure to project visually the precise and carefully drawn character concept they have in mind. Their body is their sole means of visual communication with their audience and neglecting a single visual aid will certainly lessen the possible impact of their performance. It may spell the difference between success and failure. A makeup that functions positively in helping actors project their characters is performing a service to them, the playwright, and the audience. The following article by Melvin R. White, printed in the January 1960 edition of *Players Magazine,* should be taken very seriously.

Miss Kim Stanley played the 20-year-old Irish girl, Sara Melody, in *A Touch of the Poet* during the 1958-1959 Broadway season. She used no special makeup for the roles except some mascara, letting her own idea of the girl's character project an aura of youth. *The New York Times*, Sunday, September 20, 1959, in "Gossip of the Rialto" by Arthur Gelb, stated that Miss Stanley, who hovers somewhere in the ambiguous thirties, believes in using only the barest minimum of makeup to create the illusion of either youth or age. "I think it should come from within, from the character itself," she said.

She saw no reason to resort to painted-on-wrinkles or stuffed jowls in her portrayal of the aging Collette heroine in *Cherie*. The role required Miss Stanley to age from 43 to 60, with an increase of weight from 140 pounds to 290 pounds. Her costumes were padded to add the extra weight, but her face changed without adding layers of greasepaint.

Miss Geraldine Page in *Sweet Bird of Youth* does not resort to makeup trickery in her portrayal of the aging actress in this play. She suggests years by such devices as a flabby slouch, a slack jaw, a heavy-jowled pout, a tired sag of the chin, a defeated wrinkling of the forehead, a thickly dropping eyelid, and an eye glazed with weariness.

What about the high school and college actor? Can he work with little or no makeup too? During 1958-1959 the author visited colleges and universities in 36 states, witnessing dozens of campus productions. He saw plays in community theatres. He judged two regional high school play contests. He saw some excellent makeup; he saw some atrocious makeup. Most of the time he saw much too much makeup, layers upon layers of greasepaint and lines and powdered hair trying to cover the deficiencies of young actors playing roles older than themselves and even sometimes when the actors were playing their own age. But he saw superb exceptions, too. A high school girl from Amarillo, Texas, playing Miss Prism in *The Importance of Being Earnest,* gave character and age with an unobtrusive makeup. She was being Miss Prism from within, her entire body, face, and mind became Mrs. Prism, so she did not require much makeup. A student at the University of Maryland played a mature, sophisticated society role with an indiscernible base, touches of liner on the eyes, a mere suggestion of eye shadow, and lip rouge. The extra twenty years she added to her own age came from within, from her mind, her body, her concept of the character, and not from her makeup kit.

True, a 15-year-old boy playing a 50-year-old man in a high school plays needs a greasepaint base, lines, highlights, and shadows. But *before* plastering his face with a mask, he should *be* the 50-year-old mentally, emotionally, physically, and facially, and he and his director will find that the more he grows into the role, the less makeup he will require.

How much makeup? The answer is, as little as possible.

Publicity

Publicity, including tickets, programs, and posters, is a must for each play produced. So what is needed?
- A poster to advertise the show
- The ticket to provide money to finance the production
- The program to give a preview of the production

A quick rule of thumb is to use bright colors with black ink for posters, heavy stock or light cardboard for tickets (six to eight tickets can be placed on one sheet), and regular paper for programs. Remember, have a good original copy. All the publicity you do is viewed and judged by the audience before the show has even started. You want them to be impressed, not turned off by "tacky" publicity. Freebies along the way are: TV talk shows, radio PSA (Public Service Announcements), newspaper previews, and calendars.

Set

A play can be successful and well done without the use of a set. However, depending on your performance space and resources, creating a set for your production can add yet another visual element to enhance the overall effect. Very simple scenic pieces can be created using existing items, i.e., folded-up cafeteria tables for walls, stacked boxes and crates covered with fabric for a hill, stage curtains gathered to form columns, etc. In some instances, the art department or wood shop can provide assistance with building and painting, thus involving even more students in the production.

Parents are also a great resource. A retired carpenter or painter would be invaluable if you are creating a set with limited budget. In addition, the local community college or university might offer assistance with students from their design program. It all depends on what your production calls for. Be creative — your audience has a great imagination!

Technical Terms Final Test

You must define *all* the following terms completely, not using the word to define it. Each word is worth 1 point, for a total of 10 points.

1. Counter
2. SRO
3. Monologue
4. Run
5. Upstaging
6. House
7. Shtick
8. Flats
9. Plant
10. Below

You must define *15* of the following words, not using the word to define it. Each is worth *2 points* for a total of *30* points.

1. Burlesque
2. Civic Theatre
3. Give Stage
4. Gypsy
5. Jury
6. Panning
7. Blocking
8. Apron
9. Stage Superstitions
10. Tableau
11. The Sticks
12. Trap
13. Equity
14. Focus
15. Strike
16. X
17. Ensemble

18. Ingénue
19. Quick Study
20. Repertory
21. Walk-on

Draw the acting areas of the stage, labeling each area, including the audience on the back of this page. Do not use abbreviations. Worth 20 points.

Make Up Test Technical Terms

You are only to do 40 words, each worth 1 point

1. Above
2. Call
3. Batten
4. Book
5. Character Part
6. Clear Stage
7. Ensemble
8. Flats
9. Focus
10. Give Stage
11. Green Room
12. Heavy
13. Kill
14. Pick-up Cues
15. Quick Study
16. Rake
17. Revue
18. Sitting on Their Hands
19. Featured Actor
20. Stock
21. Strike
22. Trap
23. Ad-lib
24. Aside
25. Below
26. Blank
27. Cattle Call
28. Counter
29. Cyc
30. Equity
31. Flop
32. Fourth Wall
33. Grips

34. House
35. Jury
36. Levels
37. Open Up
38. Plant
39. Repertory
40. SRO
41. and 42. Stage Superstitions
43. Steal a Scene
44. Take Stage
45. The Sticks

Draw the acting areas of the stage, labeling each area, including the audience on the back of this page. Do not use abbreviations. Worth 20 points.

Theatre Production Test

1. Explain in detail the proscenium theatre. (3)

2. Why is set the least important area of technical theatre? (3)

3. Literary worth and available talent are two of the factors in play production. What are the other two? Explain them. (4)
     1.
     2.

4. List the purposes of costumes and publicity. (8)
Costumes

Publicity

5. Renting and borrowing costumes are two ways of locating costumes. What are the other three? Explain, please. (6)
     1.
     2.
     3.

6. What were 3 points made in the video about makeup for the theatre? (3)
1.
2
3.

7. What was the purpose of the article from *Players Magazine?* (4)

8. What is put on the lights that can change moods by using colors? Explain more about this "thing." (3)

9. Floor and hand were two types of properties. What are the others? Explain. (4)

(I purposely listed 3 when the answer is only two — I am tricky that way!)

    1.

    2.

    3.

10. Why do we have publicity and why must great care be taken when working on it? (4)

11. Explain royalty, why it must be done, and everything else connected with it. (8)

12. What question didn't I ask on this test? Ask it and then answer it in detail for bonus credit. (5)

Make Up Test over Theatre Production

1. List the types of properties and something about each. (8)
    1.
    2.
    3.
    4.

2. There are four areas of "Factors in Play Production." Which is the most important and why? (2)

3. Define:
Royalty (4)
Gel (3)
Available Talent (2)

4. List the purposes of costumes. (5)
    1.
    2.
    3.
    4.
    5.

5. What is the point of the article on makeup from *Players magazine?* (4)

6. Discuss the three types of theatre. (6)
    1.
    2.
    3.

7. Why is set the least important aspect of technical theatre? (3)

8. List four purposes of lighting. (4)

    1.

    2.

    3.

    4.

9. Name three ways of locating costumes and discuss the pros and cons of each one. (9)

    1.

    2.

    3.

Choral Reading Examples

A Man Named Hods
Compiled by Nathan Howard Thorp

(This is an old Cowboy song dating from the 19th Century. It is a great one to let your students have fun with a dialect)

CHO: Come, all you old cowpunchers, a story we will tell,
2: and if you'll all be quiet, we sure will sing it well;
6: and if you boys don't like it, you sure can go to hell.
CHO: Back in the day when we were young, we knew a dude named Hods;
1: he wasn't fit for nothin' 'sept turnin' up the clods.
3: But he came west in '53, behind a pair of mules,
4: and 'twas hard to tell between the three who was the biggest fool.
1: Up on the plains old Hods he got and there his troubles began.
CHO: Oh, he sure did get in trouble — and old Hodsie weren't no man.
1: He met a bunch of Indian bucks led by Geronimo,
CHO: and what them Indians did to him, well, shorely we don't know.
2: But they lifted off old Hodsie's scalp and left him out to die,
3: and if it hadn't been for us he'd been in the sweet by and by.
CHO: But we packed him back to Santa Fe and there we found his mules,
2: for them dad-blamed two critters had got the Indians fooled.
1: We don't know how they done it, but they shore did get away,
4: and them two mules is livin' up to this very day.
5: Old Hodsie's feet got toughened up, he got to be a sport,
6: he opened up a gambling house and a place of low resort;
1: he got the prettiest dancing girls that ever could be found. —
CHO: them girl's feet was like rubber balls and they never staid on the ground.
3: And then thar come Billy the Kid,
CHO: he envied Hodsie's wealth,
2: he told old Hods to leave the town, 'twas better for his health;

4: old Hodsie took the hint and got, but he carried all his wealth
5: and he went back to New York State with lots of dinero
CHO: and now they say he's a senator, but of that we shore can't
    tell.

The Pobble Who Has No Toes
By Edward Lear

CHO: The Pobble who has no toes
had once as many as we;
when they said,
1 and 2: "Someday you may lose them all."
CHO: He replied
POB: "Fish fiddle de-dee!"
CHO1: And his Aunt Jobiska made him drink
lavender water tinged with pink [ick!]
for she said,
AUNT: "The world in general knows there's nothing so good for a
    Pobble's toes!"
CHO: The Pobble who has no toes
swam across the Bristol Channel.
3 and 4: But before he set out he wrapped his nose
in a piece of scarlet flannel.
For his Aunt Jobiska said
AUNT: "No harm can come to his toes if his nose is warm;
And it's perfectly known that a Pobble's toes
Are safe, — provided he minds his nose!"
CHO: The Pobble swam fast and well
and when the boats or ships came near him,
GIRL: he tinkledy-blinkedly-winked a bell [ding-ding]
CHO: so that all the world could hear him.
CHO 2: And all the sailors and admirals cried
when they saw him nearing the further side,
BOYS: "He has gone to fish for his Aunt Jobiska's
runcible cat with crimson whiskers!"
CHO: But before he touched the shore —
5: the shore of the Bristol Channel —

6: A sea green porpoise carried away
CHO: his wrapper of scarlet flannel! [oh-no]
7: And when he came to observe his feet
8: formerly garnished with toes so neat
9: his face became at once forlorn
CHO: on perceiving that all his toes were gone!
CHO1: And nobody ever knew, from that day to present,
whosoever had taken the Pobble's toes
in a manner so far from pleasant.
10: Whether the shrimps or crawfish gray,
11: or crafty mermaids stole them away,
CHO 2: nobody knew; and nobody knows
how the Pobble was robbed of his twice five toes!
CHO: The Pobble who has no toes
was placed in a friendly Bark,
CHO 1: and they rowed him back,
CHO 2: and carried him up to his Aunt Jobiska's Park.
CHO: And she made him a feast at his earnest wish
of eggs and buttercups fried with fish,
and she said
AUNT: "It's a fact the whole world knows,
That Pobbles are happier without their toes!"

Don't Ever Seize a Weasel by the Tail
By Jack Prelutsky

You should never squeeze a weasel
for you might displease the weasel,
and don't ever seize a weasel by the tail.

Let his tail blow in the breeze;
If you pull it, he will sneeze
For the weasel's constitution tends to be a little frail.

Yes, the weasel wheezes easily;
The weasel freezes easily;
The weasel's tan complexion rather suddenly turns pale.

So don't displease or tease a weasel,
squeeze or freeze or wheeze a weasel,
and don't ever seize a weasel by the tail, by the tail,
No don't ever seize a weasel by the tail. [4]

---

4 Poem from *Zoo Doings* © 1983 Jack Prelutsky. Used by permission of HarperCollins
Publishers.

Making Memories: How to Learn and Recall

Everyone learns in his or her own way, so do what works for you.

Of course, the age-old problems of procrastination and distraction plague nearly everyone at one time or another, whether their noses are pressed to a textbook or a computer at work or a dust cloth at home.

Improving isn't easy, but success can help put order into busy lives and stop a cycle of frustration. Too many people view good organizational and concentration skills as an innate ability that some people have and others don't. There's some truth to that. It's easier for some people to sit quietly and do their work. But concentration and memory can be improved.

External Distractions

People who have trouble memorizing often have a host of distractions they need to deal with first. External distractions are the easiest to eliminate by turning down the radio, turning off the TV, or moving to a secluded library corner instead of the center of the coffee shop.

Don't try to do too much at once. Narrow your focus and take a good look at your energy and resources versus your workload. We tend not to concentrate very well if we try to do seventeen things at once.

Avoidance

Sometimes we set ourselves up to fail — we just overtax ourselves. Don't get trapped in the "clean-house syndrome" when you have the compulsion to have a spotless home (or completing some other task) at the expense of more difficult homework or office work.

Goal Setting

Decide two or three goals, prioritize them, and begin work immediately rather than waiting for something "wonderful" to happen before starting.

Tips

Do not compare yourself or your progress to others. You will either become conceited or complacent because you compare favorably, or you'll become depressed and anxious because you don't compare favorably. Besides, setting your own goals and reaching them yourself is healthier and more productive in the long run.

- *Tackle Small Pieces:* Playwrights make things more convenient for performers by splitting the script into acts and scenes. Take advantage of this by splitting up your memorizing work into manageable pieces.
- *Word Relations:* Pick out the most important words in a sentence and find the relationship between those words. Are there rhyming words? Does the same letter repeat at the beginning of words? What links one important word to the next important word or one sentence to the next sentence?
- *Lights Out Technique:* Sit back, close your eyes, take a deep breath, and let your mind run over all of your thoughts and internal roadblocks for a few moments. Then clear the mind, relax, open your eyes, and buckle down.

Student Evaluation Form

An evaluation form for students to critique their classmates

Name ____

Please rate the selected actor in the following areas on a scale from EX (excellent), VG (very good), G (good), S (satisfactory), P (poor). Please try to be as honest as possible.

Process

Effort ____

Level of Personal Challenge and Risk-Taking   ________________

Cooperation with Everyone ____________________________________

Product

Character Development____

Energy ____

Concentration and Focus _____________________________________

Ensemble/Team Work ____

Who Were They? ____

What Was Their Objective? ___________________________________

Write at least one thoughtful sentence about the student's performance:

Character Analysis for *Spoon River Anthology*
*Remember, these people lived close to
one hundred and fifty years ago.*

Justify all your answers. (55 pts.)

Your Name ______________________________________

Character Name______________________________________

1. How old is your character and why? (Remember, the character is the age he or she was when he or she died.)

2. Is your character married, single, have children? If so, their names and ages?

3. Describe your character's home — be specific.

4. Ideally, how would your character look physically? (Include costume, hair, beard, etc. You may draw a picture or cut one out of a magazine.)

5. What personal characteristics make this person different from all the others in this play?

6. What one prop would the character have and why?

7. How does your character feel about the other people in Spoon River?

8. How does he or she feel about life? (Remember, a great deal of this has to do with environment.)

9. Answer the following about your character — these are abstract.
   List and give specific reasons. Feel free to add cutouts,
   swatches, or anything else that may help your answers.
   Color: (Someone who is sad might be the color blue.)
   Food: (Someone who is very active might be popcorn.)
   Inanimate Object: (Someone who is very strict might be an
      elm tree.)
   Car: (Someone who thinks they are "hot" might have a
      sports car.)
   Shoes: (Someone who is poor might have holes in very old,
      rundown shoes.)
   Animal: (Someone who is sneaky might be a snake.)

10. What is your character's secret?

Monologue Analysis

Name ____

Character ____

Be very specific with your answers — tell me why. All answers must be in first person, as if your character were answering the questions. (35 pts.)

1. Greatest fear (tangible or intangible)

2. Happiest moment

3. Saddest moment

4. What is your long-range goal

5. Most treasured possession

6. What is your character's secret? (Having a secret always adds a sense of mystery to a character.)

7. What color do you associate with your character? Why? (For example, you might associate a jealous character with green.)

8. What object do you associate with your character? Why? (For example, you might associate a pocket watch with a character who is a time-controlled person.)

9. What animal do you associate with your character? (For example, you might associate a sly character with a fox.)

10. Tell me five things about your family.
    1.
    2.
    3.
    4.
    5.

Analysis for Building Your Own Character

The following items are clues into any character. As you build your character you will want to know as much about him or her as possible. Use these questions as a springboard for your imagination. The more fully developed (much detail) your answers, the more interesting your character. Remember, *imagination is more important than knowledge!*

1. Name of character.
2. What is your character's job?
3. Where does he or she live?
4. What kind of clothes does your character wear?
5. What are your parents like? Do you get along with them?
6. Are you married or single? Why?
7. What are your character's best qualities? Why?
8. What are your character's worst qualities? Why?
9. What is your character's favorite food? Why?
10. What is your character's favorite sport? Why?
11. What is your character's dream vacation?
12. Does your character have children? Does he or she ever want children?
13. Has your character ever been in prison? Why?
14. What kind of an education does your character have?
15. If given $20, what would your character do?
16. Is your character a morning person? A night owl? Why?
17. Is your character lazy or energetic? Perhaps lazy about only certain things?
18. How would your character respond to an annoying sales person?
19. What kind of music does your character listen to?
20. What kind of television show does your character watch?
21. "I want ___________________________ out of life!"

Program

Bits & Pieces

A Drama 2 Production

The students wrote all of these pieces during our first quarter. The respective class chose the order and the individual pieces. We hope you enjoy our look at ourselves.

Opening Number

Period 5

I Don't Have $6.50

"Boy, you got a panty on your head"

First Kiss No Pony — No Cookies

Edu K shun

Cheating Hurts

Intermission

A B?

Rhyme Time

English 101

Sunday Morning Nap

Mother

My Journal

I Will Be Here

Parent Trap

Period 6
My First Kiss
Sonlight Singers
Oops!
Test Time
Big Trip #3
What a Horrible Time
Why … How
Pa Beasley's School of Opermatation of a Motre ve-hickl
CPR?
The Big Date
The Four Stages of Life
Gotcha
Prep for Life
Remember Me Sunshine

Finale

**Don't miss our next production
Mystery of the Black Abbot
Oct 28-29th**

Handout for Incoming Eighth Graders

Sentinel's Drama Department

What students have said about our drama classes:
Fun but challenging.
Allows everyone to be creative.
Helps overcome shyness.
Chance to interact with students on a more personal level.
You make most choices; the teacher just supervises.
Gives you confidence.
Super class for everyone to take.
Stick with it, it gets better and better.
It's different, a great way to start the day.

Curriculum
- **Drama 1 (1 Semester):** Drama 1 is an activity course with many group exercises. Most work is done in class that includes: pantomime, choral reading, technical theatre, improv, play writing, and acting. An evening performance in the Little Theatre worth 1/3 of the semester grade will be presented the last week of the semester. This elective can count as part of the fine arts requirement.
- **Drama 2 (1 Year):** Drama 2 is a play production class offered to juniors and seniors. Two major plays are presented to the public as well as shows written for the junior high and grade schools. As with Drama 1, most of the activity is done in class, stressing group work. This elective requires passing Drama 1 and can count towards junior and senior English or fulfill the fine arts requirement.

Extracurricular
- **All-School Plays:** There are two all-school plays with open auditions for any student who wants to become involved. We also have openings on crew work such as costumes, set, lights, sound, and props. Rehearsals are every Monday through Thursday from 7-9 p.m.

- **Thespian Troupe 483:** The International Thespian Society is a non-profit, tax-exempt honorary organization for high school theatre students. The society is committed to the advancement of educational theatre, publishing the *Dramatics* magazine and presenting the Montana State Thespian Convention, which provides college scholarships. The only requirements are: 100 hours on or offstage at Sentinel and an overall grade point average of 2.0. Our troupe sponsors the Sadie Hawkins dance, sells concessions at ball games, handles senior cap and gowns, and presents an improv show at *First Night* and travels to NY every two years.

End of Year Letter to Parents

Dear Mr. and Mrs. Jones,

I enjoyed having Sissi in class. I felt you needed to know how much I have also enjoyed teaching Drama 2 this year. We have achieved so much with our two major productions as well as our smaller productions. Every teacher dreams about classes that want to be there every day and are willing to do extra to get the job done. My classes have indeed done that this year.

I have watched many of my students grow up, many of whom I had as freshmen. It is with students like Sissi that our drama department has gained a fine and enviable position in the state of Montana. Thank you for sharing Sissi with me.

Sincerely,

Margaret F. Johnson

About the Author

During her thirty-seven years of teaching, Margaret produced much more than great shows. She inspired many of her students to become theatre professionals. A few of her "kids" are now nationally known Broadway actors, film stars, and backstage technicians. Among them are Kathleen McNenny, a Broadway actress; Scott Michael Campbell, a television and film actor; Tom Valach, a freelance designer in the Twin Cities; and John Shaffner, an Emmy Award-Winning Designer and from 2008-2011 Chairman and CEO of the Academy of Television Arts and Sciences (Emmys).

When Margaret retired, the high school auditorium where she taught was renamed in her honor. She continues to teach acting privately and to the over fifty crowd for MOLLI (Montana Osher Lifelong Learning Institute), as well as at the Missoula Children's Theatre Fine Arts Camp. When time permits, she accepts acting roles at the Missoula Community Theatre where she works with former students.

She served as the Montana State Thespian Director from 1972 to 1992, establishing the yearly state convention in partnership with the University of Montana. Her students performed on the main stage at two International Thespian Conferences.

She has directed over 190 productions from children's theatre to full-blown musicals like *The Music Man* with a cast of 300.

Margaret graduated from Macalester College with a B.A. in Theatre and Speech and earned an M.A. in Direction from the University of Montana.

In 2007, she was thrilled when her first book from Meriwether Publishing, dealing with producing a high school play, *The Drama Teacher's Survival Guide: A complete tool kit for theatre arts,* was published. The Midwest Book Review said, "Both experienced and beginning drama directors have easy, experience-backed tips on directing. When this book says 'complete' it means it."

When she isn't acting or teaching, she enjoys living in her restored Victorian home in Missoula with her husband of forty-six years and their "children" Sissi, a Hungarian Puli, and Daphne, a fourteen-pound domestic shorthair cat. She also enjoys blogging for Contemporary Drama:

http://contemporarydramanewsletter.contemporarydrama.com/public/blog/203097

You can visit her website, margaretfjohnson.com, for more tips and tricks.